in the same series

GOOD NEWS IN MARK introduced by Robert Crotty
GOOD NEWS IN HEBREWS introduced by Thomas Corbishley
GOOD NEWS IN GALATIANS introduced by John D. Davies
GOOD NEWS IN ACTS introduced by David Edwards
GOOD NEWS IN THE EARLY CHURCH introduced by Martin Marty
GOOD NEWS IN CORINTHIANS I & II introduced by William Neil
GOOD NEWS IN MATTHEW introduced by Pierson Parker
GOOD NEWS IN LETTERS OF PAUL introduced by David H. C. Read
GOOD NEWS IN ROMANS introduced by Joseph Rhymer
GOOD NEWS IN JOHN introduced by Douglas Webster
GOOD NEWS IN LUKE introduced by Wilfred Wilkinson

JESUS FOR MODERN MAN by David Edwards

GOOD NEWS IN REVELATION

The Revelation to John
in Today's English Version

Introduced by
VERNON SPROXTON

Collins
FONTANA BOOKS
in co-operation with The Bible Reading Fellowship

First published in Fontana Books 1977

Made and printed in Great Britain by
William Collins Sons & Co. Ltd, Glasgow

CONTENTS

TO BEATRICE

FOR HER PATIENCE AND HER HOPE

PREFACE

'Writing a commentary on *Revelation*! You must be mad! All that stuff about the four and twenty elders worshipping night and day and casting down their crowns before the throne. You have only to imagine it to see how ridiculous it is – those poor old men trying to retrieve their thrown-down crowns with dignity, and scuttling round the throne trying to keep their eyes full of wonder whilst at the same time watching for the cue for their next turn. And all the beasts, and battles, and bad women, and blood, which makes it look as though St John or whoever had just returned from a bad LSD trip or was dream-working his way through a lot of unresolved aggression. What prompts you to think that you can make sense of that lot?'

What indeed! But it is good to have candid friends, and in the months that have elapsed since the remark was made in a light-hearted way I have seen that it touches directly on the deepest problem in the writing of this commentary. For if there is *Good News in Revelation* it is embedded in a quite remarkable quantity of bad news which, on a first reading, is more easily comprehensible than the good. And I have often despaired of ever being able to restore to the last book of the Bible the spiritual and moral dynamic and excitement it must have generated in its first readers, and to do so in such a way that the prospect of receiving 'the Morning Star' makes sense to people who live in a world where men create artificial stars almost without noticing what they are doing.

Hitherto, although I knew something of the book's origin and had read and re-read several of its more popular passages, I had never applied myself to the book as a whole and in detail. Now I feel that I am able to hear something of *Revelation*'s ground-bases. The effect is tonic and invigorating. This springs not from any intellectual propositions to which the text can be reduced, but from the wonderfully resonant symbols which pile up in the imagination and engender a spirit of resolute and buoyant hilarity. Living cheek by jowl with the images and the dramatic tension of the book has worked in me a subtle but marked change, and all that I can hope to do in so short a commentary is to clear the way for the reader to be grasped by the reality in which the symbols have their ground. Further than that I do not think that we can safely go, for to construct an eschatology on the images of *Revelation* alone would be ill-advised For it will not yield to too logical an approach. That is why, as John Donne said of the doctrine of the Trinity, it may be 'bones to philosophy but milk to faith'.

I am not an academic, and have not had time to wade through the volumes and monographs which have been written on the subject. I am dependent on the spadework which others have done (marvelling at the ingenuity of the human mind in finding such diverse patterns in the same material!), and offer very little which is new except, perhaps, the insistence that the reader who struggles too hard to understand the text in a purely intellectual way will miss its meaning. That is why the Introduction is relatively long, staking out certain guidelines to enable the reader to make his own way without the incubus of too much detailed exposition. For once the general direction of John's thought has been grasped – of this I am more than ever convinced – the technical problems of verse order do not matter all that much.

I have been dependent upon the work of a good many scholars, which I have not space to set out in detail though some of the books are listed in Appendix B; and I have also been dependent upon the advice of a number of others. However, I should like to thank most of all my fellow members of the United Reformed Church in Hersham, Surrey, on whom, for a whole winter, large sections of this commentary were tried out.

November 1976 VERNON SPROXTON

INTRODUCTION

Tourists visiting the rosy-red island of Patmos, off the West Coast of Asia Minor, set in the brilliant blue of the Aegean Sea, generally arrive there by the port of Scala. They will be unable to miss the great monastery which dominates the town, and was founded in 1088 to commemorate the exile there of Saint John the Divine. They will be directed to a small cave in between the town and the harbour which is known as 'The Grotto of the Apocalypse', for it is, according to legend, the site of John's ecstatic vision.

Unless their guide is very well informed they will probably not realize that, with the possible exception of The Gospels and The Epistle to the Romans, the vision which came to John on that spot has had a greater influence on religious aspiration and political ideology than any other part of the New Testament. On the one hand it has coloured the dreams of Christians about what attends them in the eternal heavens, and on the other hand it has given authority to those who would assume The Rule of the Saints on earth.

Who was John?

Frankly, we do not know who John was. 'The divine' is an honorary title, meaning 'the preacher'. It is possible, though improbable, that when *Revelation* began to circulate, the name of a well-known saint was attached to give it weight. Most scholars agree that he was not the author of the Fourth Gospel: for one thing his Greek is bad, the worst in the New Testament; for another, the great themes of the Gospel (light and darkness etc.) are missing.

The claims John makes for himself are touchingly modest: 'A brother and companion in suffering because he had proclaimed the truth that Jesus had revealed'. It is likely, therefore, that he was a senior Christian leader of some local repute who had been exiled on Patmos.

The Life Situation

Though we know very little about the exact circumstances in which the Apocalypse was written we know a very great deal about the general conditions in which the life of the Church was set. The Church was still quite young. It had established itself in Jerusalem and Rome, and with remarkable speed and energy it had extended into Asia Minor. But it had nothing like the structure that it was to have within two or three hundred years. It consisted in a multitude of loosely-related 'associations', with virtually no property to speak of, and certainly no buildings. Moreover, its status tended to be ambiguous, and there was always the danger that persecution would break out, especially when it was seen that Christians were not a sect within Jewry (Judaism was 'protected') but a people with a distinctive life and philosophy of their own, who nourished a fervent hope that the Second Coming of Jesus was not far off.

This tension between the Church and the State was always present to a greater or lesser degree. And it is the outbreak of persecution in Asia Minor which gives us some clue about the time in which John was writing. There had been persecutions before, but only in Rome, where Christians had been blamed for the Great Fire. But only Nero and Caligula had really pressed home their claim to be worshipped as divine. However, a rumour had reached John that Nero had returned. And, as a precedent had been set for exiling and killing Christians simply because they were Christians, John feared the worst if another 'Nero' should appear. And such a man was Domitian.

The Emperor Domitian

Domitian took his divinity very seriously indeed and insisted on his Civil Service calling him 'my Lord, and my God.' He even executed close relatives for not doing him the honours. So it was clear that Christians were in for a very bad time, for to call a mere man 'Lord and God' was utterly offensive to them. And there could be no compromise between the Church and a State which had become so diabolical that it arrogated to itself powers and made claims on man, which were proper to the true God alone. So, when Christians refused to sacrifice a pinch of incense at the temple of Caesar to enable them to get a 'certificate of worthiness' at the local police station they were probably taking the first step on the road to martyrdom.

Thus, if Domitian is 'Nero returned from the dead', John is writing at about the last decade of the first century. He saw where things were going to lead and the paramount need of strengthening the faith of the timorous Christians by giving them such a vision of what God had done, was doing, and had surely promised to do, that it brightened their hopes, quickened their obedience and, above all, prevented their apostasy. For, as we shall see, in John's view, apostasy was a fate worse than death.

What is Apocalypse?

John chose a genre of literature which was familiar and ready to hand to give expression to his Big Vision. It would have been much easier for us if he had thought of something else, for though we are familiar with letters, biographies, travellers' tales, parables, and sermons, and all the other styles of writing which comprise the New Testament, we have not much of a clue about apocalypse and, apart from the Letters to the Seven Churches and a couple of chapters on the New Jerusalem, it looks as though the New Testament comes to an end on a note of incomprehensibility. Yet, in the experience of each of us there are events which hint at the meaning of apocalypse.

Most people have been present at a public function when a well-known person pulls a cord and a flag falls away to uncover for the first time a painting or piece of statuary which an artist has at last completed. Such people would be astonished if you told them that they had just witnessed an **apocalypse**. But that is the word the Greeks would have used for the event: apocalypse – the unveiling of something so far hidden from view, and thus making known something which hitherto has remained a mystery. It is this word we translate by **revelation.** Revelation in common speech still carries some of the overtones of mystery: 'More Revelations about Member of Parliament and Chorus Girl'; 'New Revelations about Income Tax Fraud'.

Unfortunately, the primary meaning of 'apocalypse' has been eroded by the company it keeps. We most frequently read it as an adjective (apocalyptic) to describe disaster, pestilence, atrocities, bloodshed, and war. And so the essence of the word, 'to uncover', is lost in the general mess of imprecision.

Mystery

We have also got to rid the word **mystery** of the notion of spookiness and the other spine-chilling associations of its present use. Its proper meaning may be seen in what happens when a new Pope is elected. The crowds wait in Saint Peter's Square, in Rome, whilst the Cardinals are locked in secret conclave to make their choice of a new Pontiff. When the white smoke billows from the chimney they know that a decision has been made. That decision is the mystery. Presently the Cardinals appear on the balcony and the Senior Cardinal Deacon, paper in hand, addresses the crowd: '*Habemas Papem* – we have a Pope'. Then he reads from the paper the name of the new Pope. The paper 'holds the mystery' which the Cardinal Deacon *reveals* to the crowd.

It is vitally important to keep in mind the precise meaning of these words: the unveiling of something that has been hidden; in this case God's plan for the completion and end of all things that are. For that is what *The Book of Revelation* is all about.

The Heart of the Matter

There are undoubtedly many difficulties in the way of understanding the book in detail, but no intelligent person who has the patience to work through it unaided can have any doubts about its general drift. However much he may be perplexed, shocked, and outraged by some of its narrative and language, its message rings out loud and clear: *the victory of God's purpose for the world, which evil has no power ultimately to frustrate*. But if he *does* find it perplexing he is in good company. Dr William Barclay tells of a professor of biblical studies who warned his students that if they were not mad before they began reading the book they would be by the time they had finished it. And it certainly has a curious hold on some of the more bizarre and fanatical sects, and provides a happy hunting-ground for parsons looking for scriptural jockeys to ride their pet doctrinal hobby-horses. But even more distinguished people, who should have known better, shied away from it. When he was translating the New Testament John Calvin had to give it up as a bad job. Luther dismissed it as small beer. More recently Rudolph Bultmann dubbed it 'weakly christianized Judaism'. Professor A. M. Hunter could only achieve *The Unity of the New Testament* by dropping it altogether.

'Imagination is the rudder'

On the other hand poets have found *Revelation* a source of inspiration. It provoked John Ruskin to tears of penitence and joy. Blake went into raptures over it. Samuel Coleridge found in it the quintessence of symbolism. Christina Rossetti used it as the basis of a monumental devotional commentary. Poets, painters and musicians have been transported out of themselves by it. And it is easy to see why artists have been moved by it when it has left theologians cold. For it approximates more to poetry than to logical discourse. It will not yield its truths to a too logical approach. It is, in a sense, a long poem, and of long poems Keats said, 'Fancy is the sails, and imagination is the rudder'. *Revelation* stands or falls by the way in which it fertilizes and grips our imagination. It is significant that one of the great recent commentaries, that of Dr Austin Farrer, was called *The Rebirth of Images*. And a purely logical approach can glean little from *Revelation*'s vibrant and powerful images.

Frames of Mind

To be quite honest, if I were asked what chance the modern reader has of receiving an exact duplicate of what John intended his original readers to understand and feel, I would rate it no higher than the chance of the Deputy Commodore of the *Queen Elizabeth* being able to share an African tribesman's experience as he paddles his canoe up the Zambesi. This is not to denigrate the tribesman. If I were lost in the jungle I would prefer his companionship to that of the Commodore, for he carries in his brain much of the gadgetry displayed on the bridge of the *Queen Elizabeth*. For both men look on life through different frames of mind. (To the African, for instance, the distinction between the individual and the group is meaningless.) And it is extremely difficult for us to shed the unconscious assumptions of Western twentieth-century man and put on the shoes and share the 'world view' of Asians living two thousand years ago. For even our knowledge of the life and times of classical antiquity has come down to us through men like Benjamin Jowett, whose minds were steeped in nineteenth-century philosophy; so that D. H. Lawrence could say, 'Plato is simply Jowett in a toga'. Lawrence had a point here. He was protesting about the way in which Christians had prevented people being reached with the powerful pagan images and symbols, by the erection of a doctrinal screen, so that man was not allowed to 'be breast to breast with the cosmos'. Certainly, there is a wide gap between the vision and prophetic rapture which is the stuff of Asian religion, and the religious experience which the average white Anglo-Saxon Protestant finds congenial and construes as, 'But it's not cricket, old man!' We must therefore try to reduce the gap to manageable proportions.

The Problems

There are basically three problems confronting the interpreter of *Revelation*.

a) *The Text*. Many battles have been fought amongst the critics, and all sorts of ingenious solutions have been proposed to solve the problems which the present order of the passages presents. Clearly some early editor worked over the initial text or texts of *Revelation* and made a botched job of it. Someone, perhaps not the same person, distorted the picture by pretending to prophesy events which had already happened. Scholars have even suggested that the book is a compilation rather than a single literary production, for in some of the visions there is neither progress of thought nor logical link. Other scholars have suggested laws which explain these clear discrepancies, like *anticipation*, where a following event is heralded in the previous scene; *undulation* where the same sequence is recapitulated in different forms; and so on. These may point to the fact that what form or order there is springs from the mind of a compiler and not from the original author, and readers who wish to know more about the subject at this stage may turn to Appendix A. But this need not necessarily detain us, for more fundamental problems lie elsewhere.

b) *Revelation and the Gospel.* Luther made clear his hesitation on this score when he wrote, in 1552, 'My spirit cannot accommodate itself to this book. There is one sufficient reason for the small esteem in which I hold it – that Christ is neither taught in it nor recognized.' Certainly it is not easy to square 'blood up to the bridles of horses' with the Son of Man riding into Jerusalem, 'lowly and riding upon an ass'. Jesus washing the feet of his disciples seems to be light years away from 'the wrath of the Lamb'. It is hard to conceive of Jesus, the quintessence of forgiveness, taking it out of his enemies, apparently more like a Sultan than a Saviour. It is therefore not astonishing to learn that when the New Testament books were put together *Revelation* came in for some rough treatment, and even then only got in by the skin of its teeth. Even today it is still treated with suspicion by the Orthodox Church, in spite of the fact that it was the pabulum of the Russian peasant in pre-revolutionary days.

These difficulties dissolve, to some degree, when we remember that although 'there is too much destroying in the *Apocalypse*. It ceases to be fun' (D. H. Lawrence), its cultural humus is not the Christianized West, but the pagan-Semitic East where, paradoxically, the religion which celebrated the necessity of unconditional forgiveness sprang from a society which had a quite remarkable penchant for grinding its enemies into the dust.

Moreover, the times called for strong stuff, and *Revelation* contains an element of rhapsody, which exults in excesses, goes too far, is not interested in half-shades any more than it is concerned for logical consistency. Thus a certain amount of cartoonery was inevitable. Rough times were ahead, and they called for quite dramatic propaganda.

c) *The Prose Barrier*. This is much the most formidable of all the problems, as Modern Man has lost the art of understanding the tools and materials with which John had necessarily to work. For he had to communicate his vision in the shape of a sustained poetic and dramatic symbol rather than literal prose, and it is just this dimension of understanding that Modern Man, for the most part, feels ill at ease with. He does understand signs. He knows that a red line drawn through a cigarette means NO SMOKING. But symbols, and images which point beyond themselves or, to put it in another way, gather round themselves clusters of meaning, resonances, and overtones, are another matter. For Modern Man suffers from a depleted and impoverished imagination; so that when he comes to a phrase like 'to those who win the victory . . . I will give the Morning Star', he blinks, puts down his bible, and turns on the television. Even if the problem of transportation could be solved (so runs his tabloid-reportage mind), who would think all those millions of tons of inert matter a sufficient reward for a lifetime's obedience?

Now, the first readers of *Revelation* never for a moment thought they were being offered a chunk of star, but they were probably much more excited by the prospect than we are. For the language of *Revelation* will not paraphrase without losing not only its impact but also its meaning. It cannot be said strongly enough that to try to précis it is to rid it of its significance.

Let us put this to the test straight away. Turn to the description of the New Jerusalem in Chapter 21 and Chapter 22, verses 1–6.

The New Heaven and the New Earth

21 Then I saw a new heaven and a new earth. The
first heaven and the first earth disappeared, and
the sea vanished. 2 And I saw the Holy City, the new
Jerusalem, coming down out of heaven from God,
prepared and ready, like a bride dressed to meet her
husband. 3 I heard a loud voice speaking from the
throne: "Now God's home is with men! He will live
with them, and they shall be his people. God himself

will be with them, and he will be their God. 4 He will
wipe away all tears from their eyes. There will be no
more death, no more grief, crying, or pain. The old
things have disappeared."
5 Then the one who sits on the throne said, "And
now I make all things new!" He also said to me, "Write
this, because these words are true and can be trusted."
6 And he said: "It is done! I am the Alpha and the
Omega, the beginning and the end. To anyone who is
thirsty I will give a free drink of water from the spring
of the water of life. 7 Whoever wins the victory will
receive this from me: I will be his God, and he will be
my son. 8 But the cowards, the traitors, and the per-
verts, the murderers and the immoral, those who
practice magic and those who worship idols, and all
liars – the place for them is the lake burning with fire
and sulphur, which is the second death."

The New Jerusalem

9 One of the seven angels who had the seven bowls
full of the seven last plagues came to me and said,
"Come, and I will show you the Bride, the wife of the
Lamb." 10 The Spirit took control of me, and the
angel carried me to the top of a very high mountain. He
showed me Jerusalem, the Holy City, coming down out
of heaven from God, 11 shining with the glory of God.
The city shone like a precious stone, like a jasper,
clear as crystal. 12 It had a great, high wall, with
twelve gates, and with twelve angels in charge of the
gates. On the gates were written the names of the
twelve tribes of the people of Israel. 13 There were three
gates on each side: three on the east, three on the south,
three on the north, and three on the west. 14 The city's
wall was built on twelve stones, on which were written
the names of the twelve apostles of the Lamb.
15 The angel who spoke to me had a gold measuring
stick, to measure the city, its gates, and its wall. 16 The
city was perfectly square, as long as it was wide. The
angel measured the city with his measuring stick: it
was fifteen hundred miles long, and was as wide and
as high as it was long. 17 The angel also measured the
wall, and it was two hundred and sixteen feet high,

according to the normal unit of measure, which he was
using. 18 The wall was made of jasper, and the city itself
was made of pure gold, as clear as glass. 19 The
foundation stones of the city wall were adorned with
all kinds of precious stones. The first foundation stone
was jasper, the second sapphire, the third agate, the
fourth emerald, 20 the fifth onyx, the sixth carnelian,
the seventh yellow quartz, the eighth beryl, the ninth
topaz, the tenth chalcedony, the eleventh turquoise,
the twelfth amethyst. 21 The twelve gates are twelve
pearls; each gate is made from a single pearl. The
street of the city is of pure gold, transparent as glass.

22 I did not see a temple in the city, because its temple
is the Lord God, the Almighty, and the Lamb. 23 The
city has no need of the sun or the moon to shine on it,
for the glory of God shines on it, and the Lamb is its
lamp. 24 The peoples of the world will walk by its light,
and the kings of the earth will bring their wealth into
it. 25 The gates of the city will stand open all day; they
will never be closed, because there will be no night
there. 26 The greatness and the wealth of the nations
will be brought into the city. 27 But nothing that is
defiled will enter the city, nor anyone who does shame-
ful things or tells lies. Only those whose names are
written in the Lamb's book of the living will enter the
city.

22 The angel also showed me the river of the water
of life, sparkling like crystal, which comes from
the throne of God and of the Lamb, 2 and flows down
the middle of the city's street. On each side of the river
was the tree of life, which bears fruit twelve times a
year, once every month; and its leaves are for the
healing of the nations. 3 Nothing that is under God's
curse will be found in the city.

The throne of God and of the Lamb will be in the
city, and his servants will worship him. 4 They will see
his face, and his name will be written on their fore-
heads. 5 There shall be no more night, and they will
not need lamps or sunlight, for the Lord God will be
their light, and they will rule as kings for ever and
ever.

The Coming of Jesus

[6] Then the angel said to me: "These words are true and can be trusted. And the Lord God, who gives his Spirit to the prophets, sent his angel to show his servants what must happen very soon."

Few people surely can remain untouched by its descriptive power in English, and no doubt it had the same effect in its original 'pidgin Greek'. But how and why does the language work? Partly because it contrasts so vividly with the cities which have become the hell-towns which form our natural habitat; but it is not entirely that. 'And I saw the holy city, New Jerusalem, coming down out of heaven from God, prepared and ready like a bride dressed to meet her husband.' Brides-cities; if we bring the images too logically together what do we get? An Englishman would vest the City Hall in something old, drape something new round the Corn Exchange, festoon the Cathedral in something borrowed, and shroud the Police Headquarters in blue. If such literal processes are applied you end up with something grotesque. And yet the picture of the New Jerusalem worked on our imagination in its own way – the way of the poetic symbol.

Poetic Symbols

So, if we are going to get the best out of *Revelation*, we must leave our logic-chopping minds behind and open our imaginations to the influence of the *poetic symbol*. It is, in fact, critical for our understanding the Bible as a whole, as Matthew Arnold was quick to point out when he wrote, '. . . the word "God" is used in most cases as by no means a term of science or exact knowledge, but a term of poetry and eloquence, a term *thrown out*, so to speak, at a not fully grasped object of the speaker's consciousness, a literary term in short . . .' (*Literature and Dogma*, 1895, p. 9). But Modern Man has become so used to scientific, descriptive reportage that poetry is the occupation of the few. He may weep to see 'the daffodils haste away so soon'; he may, indeed, try to 'fill the unforgiving minute with sixty seconds' worth of distant run'; he may even bewail that 'now you live on ribbon roads and no man knows or cares who is his neighbour'. But the following lines, which close T. S. Eliot's *Four Quartets*, will leave him bewildered:

> And all shall be well
> All manner of thing shall be well
> When the tongues of flame are infolded
> Into the crowned knot of fire
> And the fire and the rose are one.

Yet these few lines are, in my view, amongst the most beautiful, pregnant, and profound in the whole of English, leaving, as they do, a complex pattern of brilliantly resonant symbols, and allusions to Dante and Lady Julian of Norwich. They are virtually contemporary. Yet they are nearer to the world of *Revelation* than to *the Daily Telegraph*; and *Revelation* is nearer to the *Four Quartets* than it is to *St Mark's Gospel.*

Roses, Clouds and Motor Cars

The rose, with its entourage of meanings (for passionate love and Lancashire if red, for purity and Yorkshire if white) means a great deal to an Englishman; but it need not have quite the same significance for a Singhalese. He would have to do some background research, and even then the spontaneity of the symbol would not grip his imagination in the same way. Similarly, we have got to try to learn something about the symbolism used in *Revelation.* For many Western men the symbol of power or of status is a Jaguar Mark X or a large BMW; for the first-century Asian it was a white horse. White is the colour which represents the Second Coming, which is also symbolized by a cloud. So, if you clothe a figure in a white robe, sit him on a white charger, and make him appear through white clouds, though it may not do much for us, you would produce a picture which would take the ancient's breath away. And Lawrence is quite right when he says that many of the symbols used in *Revelation* stretch back into pagan times. But he is wrong in saying that they were necessarily neutered, for John had the knack of taking them over, freshening them up, and giving them new vitality by baptizing them in the service of the Christian faith.

Vision

Revelation is also Vision. Anglo-Saxons, brought up on the stiff-upper-lip tradition often find themselves surprisingly moved by vision. When, on the last night of the Promenade Concerts in London, the vast audience sings William Blake's 'Jerusalem' – almost a second British national anthem – even the most hard-boiled Briton finds himself dewy-eyed as he remembers pimply-faced, school-boy resolutions to build a better world. And even though the resolutions faded with the acne there is just sufficient emotion left for him not to dismiss the visionary as a crank, even though Vision is no longer part of his frame of mind.

The element of 'not fully grasped' is present just as much in **vision** as it is in poetic symbol. Vision is meant to be visualized, but in an imprecise way. Try to realize it, to construct it, using the vision as a working drawing and you are doomed, as I learned whilst making a TV programme on Dante. It was all very well to hold in my mind's eye a loose picture of the Seventh Heaven, but it was a different matter when I was confronted by a designer, pencil and squared-paper at the ready, saying, 'How many feet of that column do you want there, and what should be the height of this trellis here?' That is why it is quite improper to ask what the Twenty-Four Elders are doing when they are not throwing down their golden crowns. (The only picture I know of this is an illumination in the Bamberg MS where the elders look absurd, as though they are playing quoits, and so shifty that they must be cheating!) And it does not matter that in John's picture of the New Jerusalem there is no Temple, whilst his Letters to the Seven Churches say there is. He is a seer and not a cost-accountant. He is not out to design a film set, but to evoke religious power. And minds open to poetic vision, like Coleridge for whom *Revelation* was the highest expression of poetic sublimity, may, like him, experience the vision as potency within.

Dreams

If Modern Man tends to be sceptical about such potency, he should take to heart what T. S. Eliot wrote in his essay on Dante. 'We have nothing but dreams and we have forgotten that seeing visions – a practice now relegated to the aberrant and the uneducated – was once a more significant, interested, and disciplined kind of dreaming. We take it for granted that our dreams come from below; possibly the quality of our dream suffers in consequence.' (*Dante*, Faber, p. 15)

That was written forty years ago. Now we have a generation which is open to modes of knowledge other than simple fact-finding. The 'counter-culture' insists that there is another order of truth than that described by scientists, and dimensions of knowledge which are beyond the range of quantification and the verifiable. But Modern Man is so immured in the fact-stating tradition that it is hard for him to grasp that it is but one gateway to knowledge amongst many. 'It is only in recent times, and largely under the growing dominance of the empirical sciences in Western culture, that the realm of facts has been limited to the verifiable. When the Australian Aboriginal speaks of his "dream times", when his rituals and patterns of life were laid down by his ancestors, he would be baffled by the apparently simple question, "Did things really happen like that?" He has simply not got the interest in empirical details to be concerned with what verifiable events occurred. For him, we might say, the real is the significant, the meaningful; so that many empirically ascertainable happenings, since they are trivial and insignificant, are less real than his cult beliefs.' (*The Concept of God*, Keith Ward, Blackwell, p. 75) Now if we are to get the best out of *Revelation* we have to lose our prejudice that only the verifiable is true and place our feet firmly in the shoes of those who understand Reality as the perception of the Significant. For *Revelation* is significant dream.

Ecstasy

When we raise the question of the nature of the vision we begin to skate over very thin ice. John says (1:11) quite simply that whilst he was in the Spirit of the Lord's Day he was told to write down in a book what he saw. He at any rate was convinced that he had been in some sort of ecstatic state. How it came about we do not know: hunger, anxiety, deprivation – who can tell? No doubt the main theme of the vision had been on his mind. No doubt much of the vision was worked over and elaborated. But there is frankly no reason why a substantial part of what he recorded should not have been dreamt. Coleridge dreamt the whole *Kubla Khan*, a poem which would have been much longer if a tradesman had not interrupted him whilst he was writing it up the following morning!

The word *ecstasy* stems from a Greek root (*ek-stasis*) and carries the notion of standing outside oneself. It does not necessarily mean the state of complete unity with the divine of which mystics sometimes speak. It is much more accurately represented by expressions such as 'the privileged moment', or 'the moment of expanded consciousness' which is a common enough aspect of contemporary literature and has been experienced by writers as different as Yeats, Sartre, and Simone Weil. All these were at times transported out of themselves for a time before being brought down to earth with a bump. And even the hard-boiled rationalist, Plato, has flattering things to say about what the French call *jeux d'ésprit*. 'Only through the demonic is there intercourse and conversation between men and gods, whether in the waking state or during sleep, and the man who is expert in such work is a demonic man, compared with whom the experts in arts or handicrafts are but journeymen.' (Symposium, 202D) So it looks as though in classical times, and after all John was much nearer to them than we are, such dreamers were regarded as aristocrats of the spirit. There is therefore no ground for minimizing the importance of John's vision because it came to him in a state of ecstasy. If he was beside himself he was so to good purpose.

Not Allegory

Assuming then that in *Revelation* we have in substance the content of a dream or trance, we must be on our guard against opposite dangers. Firstly, we must not think of it as we think of Dante's *Divine Comedy*, or Milton's *Paradise Lost*, where the images are under tight control and the symbols are precise. *Revelation*'s grammar is all over the place. It is discursive. It is inconsistent. You can never say 'got it', because it is not allegory. 'The true symbol defies all explanation, and so does the true myth. You can give meaning to either – you will never explain them away. Because symbol and myth do not only affect us mentally, they move the deep emotional centres every time. The great quality of mind is finality. The mind understands and there's an end of it . . . But the emotional consciousness of man has a life and movement quite different from mental consciousness. The mind knows in part, in part and parcel, with a full stop after every sentence. But the emotional soul knows in full, like a river in flood.' These sentences from D. H. Lawrence are of quite capital importance for us. And it may seem ungracious (especially as I have not totally avoided the error myself), but it seems to me that many commentators who have greatly enriched my understanding of *Revelation* have brought to their work too much *finality* of mind, and presumed finality in the mind of John. That is why I argue here that *Revelation* may yield more emotional truth if it is read straight through at one sitting than over a longer period with the help of a line-by-line commentary.

And not Freud either

Nevertheless, we must guard against thinking that the origin of the visions is from below, and that they are not disciplined into literary significance. Any psychologist worth his couch knows that very often dreams open up in the mind of his patient terrible abysses which produce dream-material which defy his understanding. The material presents, under symbol, reality situations which are too painful for the patient to face, and it is the analyst's job to help the patient first understand and then face the reality behind the symbols. If the patient is a poet the analyst may be able to help him say his piece. Undoubtedly John's life-situation was such that it made for nightmares. But if there is a hint here and there that the vision originated in the conflicts and anxieties of his unconscious, it is equally clear that he is trying to express what he saw in a form which is coherent, if not consistent, and intelligible, if not logical.

The Form of the Book

The nature of that form and its various aspects goes to the heart of our understanding of the vision. For though its language is poetic, symbolic, and visionary, its subject is history or, more precisely perhaps, time. John is clearly speaking about what is going to happen in history on the strength of what has happened and is happening. *Revelation* is about events. Now, speaking out, or telling forth, or interpreting events by reference to God's nature and order ('Thus saith the Lord') was almost uniquely the function of the biblical prophet. The prophet was not an astrologer, a fore-teller, but a forth-teller. He did not read the stars but the signs of the times. The editor, or whoever wrote the prologue, had no doubt about the prophetic nature of the vision. 'This book is about what Jesus Christ revealed, which God gave him, to show God's servants what must happen very soon. Christ made these things known to his servant John, by sending his angel to him, and John told all that he had seen.'

Prophecy and Portents

Revelation, then, being prophecy, is concerned with the here and now of history, but with the particular details of no epoch except the one in which it was written. Such references to historical circumstances, and they are by no means easy to identify, relate to the contemporary Roman Empire. Yet, at the same time, by looking at the events of his own day against the back-drop of God's plan for the world, John's vision has implications for the historical process as a whole, its meaning, and its End. That is why J. B. Phillips rightly says that the reader is 'carried, not into some never-never land of fancy, but into the Ever-ever land of God's eternal Values and Judgements'.

None the less, people have always been ready to see portents of their own times prefigured in *Revelation*. In its day Babylon has been Rome, London, Prague and

New York. The Beast has been Nero, Mahomet, the Pope, and Hitler. T. B. Macaulay once amusingly disposed of such silliness. He had recently arrived in Mysore. 'There I found an Englishman who, without any preface, accosted me thus. "Pray, Mr Macaulay, do you not hold that Bonapart was the Beast?" "No, Sir, I cannot say that I do." "Sir, he was the Beast, I can prove it. I have found the number 666 in his name. Why, Sir, if he was not the Beast, who was?" This was the puzzling question, and I am not a little vain of my answer. "Sir," I said, "the House of Commons is the Beast. There are 658 members in the House; and these, with their chief officers, the three clerks, the Sergeant and his deputy, the chaplain, the librarian, and the door-keeper – make 666!" '

More seriously, though, efforts to identify *Revelation* with any other time, especially when they nourished the hopes of the disenfranchised and disenchanted, have generally ended in disaster. The rule of the Saints produced some bloody smudges on the pages of history. It is always dangerous to assert that what was specifically referring to *then* specifically refers to *now*. John was, after all, speaking from and to a local situation. But the assumptions of what he was trying to say there and then, the perspective which he draws, and the theological foundations on which he builds, have far-reaching consequences for the role of the Church in any place and at any period.

The Sense of an Ending

One of the assumptions which he used in projecting his great vision of what is happening to the whole process of history is an assumption which, increasingly, Modern Man is beginning not to share, for our attitudes to the long march of history are subtly changing. This was pointed up in an article by J. B. Priestley on current television drama. 'A great weakness of many new plays and documentaries is, to my mind, their persistent lack of shape. They seem to have no idea of a beginning, a middle, and an end, and it is just as if an instinctive feeling for shape, common enough in my own generation, is fast disintegrating.' (*The Listener*, December 25th, 1975)

Priestley calls his feeling for shape 'instinctive'. He may well be right. There may be something in our genes which makes us perceive life as beginning, middle, and end.

Professor Frank Kermode, in a fine book which bears directly on our theme, says that 'we are at a moment in history when it is harder than ever to accept precedents of sense-making – to believe that any earlier way of satisfying one's need to know the shape of life in relation to the perspectives of time will suffice . . . In this respect, it makes little difference, though it makes some, whether you believe the age of the world to be six thousand years or five thousand million years, whether you think time will have a stop or that the world is eternal; there is still a need to speak humanly of life's importance in relation to it – a need in the moment of existence to belong, to be related to a beginning and an end.' (*The Sense of an Ending*, Oxford, 1967, p. 3f)

This deeply-felt need to belong to some dramatic shape of life Kermode calls 'the sense of an ending'. The prophets had it in a big way and, confirmed by the Christian tradition in many ways, it has confirmed a pattern of expectancy on the cultural schemas of the Western world. It is reflected in an insistence that every form of fiction (novel, short-story, play, cartoon) ends by getting somewhere.

Stop, but no End

But, as Kermode avers, there is an anxiety about the old perspectives which eat at the heart of Modern Man so that, as R. M. Rilke put it:

> We are not reliably at home
> in the interpreted world.

For the old framework is passing and it is being substituted by a new genre of fiction, known as the 'anti-novel', which simply gets nowhere. The novels of Alain Robbe-Grillet, for instance, just start and stop. They could stop at any time. Here and there hints are dropped that some kind of purpose and meaning is to be disclosed; but, no, they mean nothing. You are no farther forward. There is no beginning, middle, and end. It could be the same with history – just one damned thing after another!

This means that the reader, if he is going to step into the shoes of those who read *Revelation* for the first time, has not only got to forget many of his prejudices and open his imagination; he has at the same time to be grasped by the strongly marked 'sense of an ending', that history, under God, is going somewhere, indeed towards some great End for which he has designed it. For, unlike the Greeks whose Golden Age was in the past, the men of the Bible did not see history as a cycle of continuously-returning epochs. They thought of it not as a circle, but as a straight line, a roadway which was going in one direction. They could not conceive of things just going on for ever and ever. And that is why the men who ultimately decided that, whatever the difficulties, *Revelation* should go into the Bible, were following in the footsteps of the prophets. You can almost hear one of the Fathers saying, 'But we must have a strong number to finish with; we simply can't let the whole thing end with *Jude*!'

It is virtually impossible for people today to be really possessed and gripped by the biblical notion that history began by God's word in Creation, was sustained and interpreted by his prophetic Word, which had been made flesh in Jesus; and would be brought to an End in a way which was consistent with his Word. But their confidence in the future was really rooted in their experience of the past. Just as the prophets looked confidently towards the future because the Israelites had been delivered at the Red Sea, so the early Christians looked confidently towards the End, sooner rather than later, because they believed that their destiny had been settled by the triumph of Jesus over death, the most significant moment of the Christian Past.

The Death of the Past

The Past with a capital P! It is just here that we have more 'mind-framing' to do if we are really to stand in John's shoes. We must distinguish between history as a record of what has gone on in previous ages and in which one event leads to another, and a Past which contains significant events and interpretations which combine to give meaning to the present and direction to the future. It can perhaps be fairly said that Modern Man knows only the first, whilst John knew only the second, and that most Christians waver somewhere in between. In any event the notion of the Past is losing ground.

Professor Plumb, in a luminous book, puts the situation very clearly. 'The death of the past does not deny a future for history. For each one of us is an historical being, held in a pattern created by Time, and to be unconscious of our historical selves is fraught with dangers. History, however, is not the past. The past is always the created ideology with a purpose, designed to control individuals, or motivate societies, or inspire classes. Nothing has been so corruptly used as concepts of the past. *The future of history and historians is to cleanse the story of mankind from those deceiving visions of a purposeful past.*' (*The Death of the Past*, Pelican, p. 16. Italics are mine.)

Now Judaism and Christianity have both visions of a purposeful past and a meaningful future. No doubt, as Plumb hints, they have sometimes been used deceitfully. But they are of the very essence of the Christian faith. No doubt the Christian claim that the life of one man (and of that only a couple of years, and of those two years principally one week, and of that week critically a few hours) gives meaning and shape to all history, must appear to many people hideously presumptuous and muddle-headed. But to suggest to John, or indeed any of the early churchmen, that there was anything wrong or perverse with it would have left him gasping with amazement. For he shared the Early Church's view that in Jesus the whole process of history had come to its end and fulfilment. He says as much when he writes: 'I am the Alpha and the Omega, says the Lord God, "the one who is, who was, and is to come".' That is the locus of the true Christian vision of a purposeful past, without belief in which *Revelation* cannot possibly make sense. But Modern Man, who regards history as a succession of events related to each other but to no ultimate purpose, can only regard this claim as the crowning absurdity.

The Origin of Apocalyptic

It was just this tension between confidence that God had got things in hand on one side and the existential evidence that things were in a bad way on the other that produced, roughly in the period between the Testaments, a unique sort of writing which sprang from despair and impatience. We know it as *apocalyptic*. The Jews were tired of waiting for the Day of the Lord, but they were convinced that if God were God he would vindicate his name. The worst of it was terribly vindictive and looked for a smashing of their enemies and their own exaltation; the best saw their hope enshrined in God's nature. Eschewing the idea that the Kingdom was going to come by nations and men accommodating their behaviour to the Divine Will, they looked for a direct intervention of God's power – a breaking into history. A student of the sociology of literature would see apocalyptic writing as the product of despair, of a people who had seen hope after hope fade away, and even the prophets leave the scene. The fulfilment of the apocalyptic dream usually centred on a divine being who would spearhead the attack on the last redoubts of evil and wickedness. As these were usually conterminous with the political oppressors it was fairly heady and dangerous stuff, and frequently written in obscure language which only communicated to people 'in the know'; so that an apparently innocent sign could carry quite lethal meanings.

And so, when the Christians became impatient with the postponement of Christ's second coming there already existed a kind of literature which had only to be modulated with their own language, and suffused with their own hopes.

Hope in the Midst of Despair

Whatever else the apocalypses may have been, they were certainly affirmations of hope. They were tracts for tough times. Against the background of despair they nourished the hope of a new world where the righteous would come into their own. 'The words of the blessing of Enoch, wherewith he blessed the elect and righteous, who will be living in the day of tribulation, when all the wicked and godless are to be removed.' (The Book of Enoch, 1:1) *Revelation* shares this hope, but from a different ground. Put quite simply it is a poetic and dramatic exposition of two texts: *Christ our hope* (1 Timothy 1:1) and *Christ in you the hope of glory* (Colossians 1:27; both Revised Version). It is a hope rooted in what Jesus has done in his victory over the powers of evil which, in principle at least, has delivered man from bondage to *the world*, that is the world as understood by St John's Gospel, as mankind in so far as it is organized in opposition to God's will. 'To those who win the victory I will give the right to sit by me on my throne as I have been victorious and now sit by my Father on his throne.' (11:21)

The Faith and Hope of John of Patmos

Everything John has to say is grounded on his belief that the victory of Jesus was the decisive encounter between the forces of good and evil. He broods on its meaning for his own situation, and for world history. He sees that, in winning the decisive battle, Jesus has fulfilled the Old Testament prophecies, and has brought history to its fulfilment or End. Some sort of analogy may be found from the Second World War. When the Russians had driven the Germans from Stalingrad, and the Allies had hurled them out of North Africa, there could then be no doubt about the outcome of the war, though years were to pass, and thousands of lives were to be lost in a gigantic 'mopping up' operation before the final victory could be proclaimed. John's hope centres on a conviction that because of what Jesus has done there can be no doubt about God's final victory over the forces of darkness and evil, though the mopping-up operation will go on, and in it the martyrs have their own proper place. That hope is the thread which runs through all the diverse parts of his vision, and to reveal the splendour of what is in store – to uncover the mystery – is the urgent purpose of *Revelation*.

The Sources of the Vision

What we have before us is not the vision itself, but John's reported memories. He was conscious that the Spirit was the cause of what he saw, but he was not writing at the

Spirit's dictation. No doubt he had to brood on, and work over, the large amount of material he was given, perhaps even subtly altering its meaning to suit his purpose. We can have a rough idea of what his sources were.

1. *The Old Testament.* John's mind was steeped in the imagery and history of the Chosen People. The Old Testament was the only 'bible' the early Christians had. D. T. Niles calculated that, spread over the four hundred and four verses of *Revelation*, there are five hundred and eighteen allusions to the Old Testament. Virtually all the big themes are backed with, if not suggested by, the Old Testament. Therefore it is, as he says, 'of immense significance that the last book of the Bible should be one in which the scriptures come to a glowing re-statement, in which allusion is heaped upon allusion, vision is fused with vision, and echo with echo, until there is a procession of ideas, figures, and events which assault the imagination, awaken memory, and captivate the soul.'

2. *The symbols of Jewish apocalyptic.* We know now that there were many apocalypses circulating at the time, and these formed a real quarry of materials and no doubt carried the overtones of a much older and deeper symbolism from their origin in pagan antiquity: dragons, horsemen, beasts, blood, thunder, lightning, plagues. Perhaps too much emphasis has been put on the 'code' function of these symbols by Modern Man, with his desire for logical and consistent meanings. It is likely that for the ancient, who was much less intellectual, they would act as 'triggers' for deep-seated emotional responses.

3. *Angels. Revelation* contains a well-developed angelology, which some Christians may find offensive, because the rest of the New Testament reveals that Jesus Christ is sufficient a High Priest to mediate between man and God. But it must be remembered that angels appear in both the Old Testament and apocalyptic literature and that, in making a highly dramatized picture of the End, John badly needed some convention for communicating between Earth and Heaven. The notion of a mediating angel admirably filled the bill. It is, however, difficult for us to visualize them when our notions of angels are

haunted by the memory of boys and girls dressed up as sub-fairies with lop-sided wings for the annual nativity play! The German poet, R. M. Rilke, wrote a great deal about angels and, though his admirers will quickly point out that he did *not* mean Christian angels, his angels perform a quasi-religious function and J. B. Leishman interprets Rilke's angel as '. . . a being in whom the limitations and contradictions of present human nature have been transcended . . . both an inspiration and a rebuke, a source of consolation and also a source of terror; for while he guarantees the validity of man's highest aspirations and gives what Rilke calls "direction" to his heart, he is at the same time a perpetual reminder of man's immeasurable remoteness from his goal.' (*The Duino Elegies*, p. 102)

That is a good way to think about John's angels. They are more than message-boys. Whether or not they exist does not matter – though they are, in fact, a part of Catholic and Protestant belief – for their 'fictional' use is justifiable.

4. *The Daily Life of the Church.* John also uses familiar parts of the domestic life of the early Church: fragments from the early liturgies, such as the great hymns which are familiar to us from the oratorios of Handel and Haydn:

> Lord God Almighty,
> How great and wonderful are your deeds!
> King of all nations,
> How right and true are your ways. (15:3–4)

And it also looks as though he incorporated teaching from an early catechism which was founded on words like *watch, resist, put off the old, put on the new.*

5. *Secret Numbers.* By far the most puzzling part of his vision, however, is his use of numbers, his arithmology. The use of number as symbol was popular in the ancient world. Seven was the symbol for perfection; six, which falls short by one, i.e. 'sins', was the symbol for sin. So 666 is Sin Writ Large or The Beast. There is also evidence, especially in the architecture of the New Jerusalem, that he was aware of the canon of proportion which stemmed from a sacred geometry, and which reputable critics have

also found in such buildings as Chartres.

6. *Topography*. It is principally in his Letters to the Seven Churches that John makes use of allusion to the towns' peculiar histories, buildings, trades, and institutions. Doubts have sometimes been expressed about the importance of these, but they appear so consistently in his Letters that it looks as though he may be using them to underline the particularity of each situation. And, in any case, all communicators know that there is nothing like a concrete, local reference to drive a point home!

The Great Drama

From materials such as these then, John constructs his great drama of the things that are about to come to pass: the titanic clash of forces, the thousand years' rule of Christ, the Second Coming, the End of all things, a world restored. The range and breadth of his vision is magnificent, at times breathtaking.

But his timing was quite wrong. These things did not come to pass. Two thousand years have nearly come and gone. Things are much the same as they were. Until quite recently Christians were quite happy to keep on pushing the date back. As Frank Kermode points out, 'the great majority of interpretations of Apocalypse assume that the end is pretty near. Consequently historical allegory (that is, whether the Beast is the Pope, Mahomet, or Nixon) is always having to be revised; time discredits it. And this is important. Apocalypse can be disconfirmed without being discredited. This is part of its extraordinary resilience.'

Why the Delay?

It was not very long after the *Revelation to Saint John* appeared that time began to discredit it. Some scholars explain the great apostasies of the second century by the disappointment which prevailed amongst Christians when the New Heaven and the New Earth did not appear. For the delay made them look ridiculous. 'They will make fun of you and say, "He promised to come, didn't he? Where is he?" Our fathers have already died but everything is the same as it was since the creation of the world.' (2 Peter 2:3–4) That was probably written in the second century and though the author goes on to affirm that the Day will still come, it is clear from the rest of the letter that his mind is tinged with eschatological despair, and that the continuation of history – 'the same as it was since the creation of the world' – is puzzling Christians.

Truth to tell, the End, and how to interpret and understand it, remains to this day one of the most baffling problems of New Testament study. For there is no hard and fast New Testament line on the subject. What evidence there is assumes the character of those optical illusions which can be interpreted as either profiles of faces looking at each other, or a Greek urn. What you see depends on your prejudice; but the figure is not either/or; it is both/and. The teaching of the New Testament on the End is of the same order. No doubt the Asian mind was not as bothered by the paradox as ours is, for we are being conditioned by contemporary science to read information in computerized ways in the binary form, that is either 'on' or 'off'. Both 'on' *and* 'off' scares us.

So we have no alternative but to accept that in the New Testament we get the reverse and obverse faces of the same coin. One face presents the End as in the future, and history as the setting of the last act of the drama in which Christians can work out their apprenticeship – or what Saint Irenaeus called 'the Church's pedagogy'. The other face shows the End as having already taken place. The New Age is already with us and the signs of its presence are the New Creature, and Life in the Spirit.

The Now and the Not Yet

The problem would not go away even if *Revelation* were dropped from the New Testament. For both notions live together in the Gospels. Jesus talks about the *coming* reign of God yet, in a strange way, the reign is regarded as *already present* in him. He teaches his followers to pray for the coming of the Kingdom, but when asked 'When?' he replies that the exact time is in God's hand, for its coming is independent of anything man can do. And again, as Dr C. H. Dodd has shown us, the New Testament proclaims both the coming of the Kingdom and its charismatic presence in Jesus (what he calls 'realized eschatology' – or The Last Things made present), which constitutes a challenge to those who have the insight to see its significance.

Of and Not Out of the World

The teaching of St Paul is no more consistent. There is the *apocalyptic* element in which he contemplates history as the Not Yet, a time of preparation for the in-gathering of the Gentiles; and there is the *existentialist* element which dwells on fulfilment in the Now. 'When anyone is joined to Christ he is a new being; the old has gone, the new has come.' (2 Cor. 5:27) He was able at one and the same time to exclaim 'to live is Christ; to die is gain'.

It is probably only in the Gospel of St John that the apocalyptic element fades and the emphasis is placed on the Now: 'now is the judgement of this world', and 'unless a man eats the body of the Son of Man he is not really alive at all'.

So, by and large, *Revelation* is in step with the rest of the New Testament. A New Age has dawned in Jesus, a being in whom the ages find their fulfilment, and a New Age begins when a man surrenders himself to the will of Jesus and loves his neighbour. The Christian then, though not *of* this world, is *not out of* this world. He may, in one sense, be beyond Time; but he still lives in Time. He is at once enmeshed in history and transcends it. That is the best sense we can make of the two faces of the End for, as Dr George Steiner has pointed out, no language has a grammar which can clearly articulate the experience of Christian faith.

The Curtain Falls

In a way this relieves the Christian from the necessity of fretting about the Finish for, whether the creation lasts for six thousand or six thousand million years, some day there will be a Stop. Whether it goes out with a bang or a whimper is quite beside the point. There is good biblical authority for a Final Day (Luke 21:35) which only God knows (Mark 13:32). And the advice of Jesus is to be always watching for it. Once we have set the message of *Revelation* within the context of biblical theology we see that, beyond its immediate pastoral purpose, which was to nourish the wavering Christians in a time of trouble, it is a celebration of Christ as the One who came, comes, and shall come. Though the End can only stand at the end of the process, it prophetically says something about, and is being realized within, the process. The problem which so obsessed Søren Kierkegaard, how an historical event – the life and death of Jesus – could both make for present authenticity and become the ground of expectancy, is one which finds some answer if we take a wide view of *Revelation*. In fact the whole sequence of visions, horrifying, breathtakingly beautiful, turbulent, serene – the vast complex tapestry of saga and symbol – makes no sense unless it is set within the framework of this wide, ultimately sacramental view of what John was trying to say. For just as the End is made present in the Eucharist, Judgement Day is both now and not yet. In this tension the Christian is called to live his life.

Revelation should therefore be a tonic, for its underlying message is clear: the meaning and end of history is Jesus Christ. Modern Man with 'his need in the moment of existence to belong' is faced with Christ Crucified and Glorified, an object not of knowledge but of faith, a faith which takes bitterness out of tragedy, reduces catastrophe to proportion and, without showing him the distant future, gives him sufficient light and bearing to tackle with resolution the task that lies immediately to hand.

Breast to Breast with the Cosmos

But more. Such a hope, transcending the limits of logic, evokes a spirit of exaltation which gives man back to the cosmos. Lawrence may have been right in saying that *Revelation* was used as a threat in the ranting Methodist Chapels when what was needed was something 'to re-establish the living organic connections with the sun, and with the earth, with mankind'. But he was wrong in not realizing that this is precisely what *Revelation* does. For, as far as we can see, the one Epistle that John appears to have known is the Epistle to the Colossians which is, above all, a hymn of praise to the cosmic Christ, in whom all things in heaven and earth are gathered together. Christ, as Teilhard de Chardin was always insisting, is the middle term by which man connects with the cosmos, and through which, to those with imagination, such apparently unpromising gifts as the Morning Star open up exhilarating prospects of man's place in a Creation Restored.

Nor is there anything pagan about such a hope, but it is largely the poets who have sung about it; Coleridge for instance:

> Know, then, thyself! Expand thy wings divine!
> Soon, mingled with the fathers thou shalt shine
> A star amid the starry throng,
> A God the Gods among.

And it was the Christian poet, Norman Nicholson, who could write:

> My ways are circumscribed, confined as a limpet
> To one small radius of rock; yet
> I eat the equator, breathe the sky, and carry
> The great white sun in the dirt of my finger nails.

Back to Earth

The reader may well say that it is all very well to have these imaginative flights into poetic fancy, but what has *Revelation* to offer to the Church on earth where men often use apocalyptic language to describe a near future, with the prospects of a nuclear Armageddon, famine, global pollution, genocide, and life under political tyrannies; or, even at best, an era of continued anxiety in which life is stripped of significance or ultimate meaning, and people live together in hell-towns bereft of vital symbols and celebration?

Firstly, it is realistic. It does not minimize the magnitude of man's rebellion against God. Nor does it soften the picture of what happens when man departs from the law of love and worships that which is less than God. It is hard and completely unsentimental. It entertains no empty hopes that some edifying slogan, or resolution of the World Council of Churches, or an Archbishop's Call to the Nation, will match the hour and be equal to the deeply tragic dimensions of a world such as ours.

Secondly, it gives the Church, in a time of complacency, a prophetic role, so that it can anticipate, understand, and announce the moral consequences of a materialism which is idolatrous. And yet, equally, and at the same time, when mankind is enmeshed in a period of break-up and catastrophe, it gives the Church grounds for offering a word of hope contingent on repentance. For almost right up to the end the grim future it portrays is 'a conditional future'. *Revelation* thus speaks of judgement and of grace.

Lastly, it affirms that though the Final Victory is with God and with God alone, there is a multitude of contingent, small victories for which man is responsible, and for which he must strive. For, in a not-easily-defined way the martyrs have a vital part to play in the scenario of the great drama. This means that the Church is never nearer to the thought of *Revelation* than when it is hurt and bleeding.

COMMENTARY

Notes on the Text

Readers with some knowledge of the biblical criticism relating to *Revelation* may accuse me of hedging on many of the problems it has revealed: editorial comments, crude dislodgement of verses, and soon. They may go on to charge me with blissful indifference to the literary shape: the so-called 'sets of seven', the catenas of woes and blessings, the liturgical overtones.

Certainly these are important, but there are two reasons for not paying much heed to them. Firstly, too much discussion of critical problems would get in the way of what I take to be my main task, which is to set free the main message of *Revelation* without burdening the reader with too much marginally significant information. And on the question of literary style, we are really spoiled for choice, so many, so varied, and so ingenious are the structures which from time to time different scholars have proposed. But, secondly, and more substantially, there is no way by which the present text of the book can be altered or divided into different sections, and confusion would be worse confounded if the divisions of the commentary were at variance from those of the text itself.

It is only when we come to the end of the book that real difficulties crop up. The order of the concluding chapters has faced critics with notorious problems. The great R. H. Charles could make sense of them only by a radical redistribution of the verses. Others detect two separate cities: one the Millennial City, used during the reign of Christ on earth, thus explaining the presence of unredeemed men, and the Eternal City, which stands beyond time. Others hold that there are two different versions of the same New Jerusalem brought together by an editor who was not quite up to the task. Yet others hold that Chapter 22:1–5 forms a separate description of Paradise.

Some of these proposed 'divisions', and the arguments

used for them, spring from a too-western frame of mind, on the one hand looking for a consistency which is not there, because inconsistency did not bother the asian writer and, on the other, tending to treat the language as allegory rather than allusive symbol. For instance 'wall' need not necessarily mean *barrier*, so there is no need to throw people into a frenzy by asking them who the walls keep out when there *is* no outside. It could just stand for security.

In a short work such as this it is impossible to give anything but a brief exposition of the leading ideas. Readers who wish to know more about the text are referred to Appendix A; and those wishing to explore in more detail the rich symbolism will find longer and fuller commentaries listed in Appendix B.

It is therefore only necessary to add that in my view scholars who think that the concluding chapters are a conflation of two separate pictures of the Eternal City are working on the right lines and it is for that reason that I examine the specifications of both descriptions under one heading.

Readers may find it most useful to read a section, then read the commentary, and then re-read the section.

Introduction 1:1–3

An urgent note is sounded straightaway. *Revelation* does not consist in or originate from a collection of pious musings put together by John during his exile, but in the command of Jesus Christ. He is its ground and authority. John, true to the traditional stance of a prophet, is proclaiming, 'Thus said the Lord . . .' The vision was of divine origin. Through an angelic intermediary – echoing the way the Old Testament 'distanced' God's holiness from man's creatureliness – John, God's servant (lit. 'slave'), was enabled to report the divine message which Jesus both spoke and was. It is therefore critical; firstly, because when God addresses man it is always a crisis situation: man is called upon to decide; and, secondly, because time is short and it will not be long before the 'prophetic message' is realized. But for those who respond positively to the crisis there is hope: those who 'read' the message ('aloud' and thus presumably to the church) and those who 'obey what is written' will receive a blessing. (Daniel 2:25–30)

Greetings to the Seven Churches 1:4–8

There now follows a magnificent overture, a kind of apocalypse in miniature which, like the overture to an opera, hints at the themes and *motifs* which are later going to be orchestrated. It begins and ends with a mighty affirmation of the sovereignty of God who was, who is, and is to come (Exodus 3:14), who is the eternal presence over against which and in which all the contingencies of history have their being. It is this One who is eternally present who was on earth in Jesus (God's giving of himself which is 'grace') and whose faithfulness and obedience restored relationships between God and man (which is 'peace'). So, being given authority over the 'kings of earth' with which, if John has read the signs aright, his Church, 'a kingdom of priests', will soon be embroiled. But these man-made gods will live to see the victory of the *God made man* in a show of omnipotence (alpha and omega, the first and last letters of the Greek alphabet, thus the Beginning and the End) which is not rooted 'in the power of unlimited coercion but the power of invincible love' (Caird).

There were, of course, more than seven churches in Asia; but seven was a mystic number, denoting completion, and is probably used to suggest that though John wrote to the peculiar conditions of each church, the 'wretchedness and greatness' of which he clearly knew, the collection of letters is representative of the whole Church. (There was, it appears, a vogue in collected editions of letters, springing from a set of seven of Paul's letters which were in circulation at the time.)

A Vision of Christ 1:9–20

There had been no vigorous persecution of Christians in Asia, but since Nero's time they had lost the security and protection they enjoyed when they were able, as an apparent sect within Jewry, to avail themselves of the exemption allowed the Jews in respect of emperor-worship. But that was in Rome. In Asia things were different. No magistrate could start proceedings unless a complaint had been laid before him, and then what happened to the offender was entirely in his hands. Someone must therefore have 'told on' John, for he found himself exiled on Patmos for proclaiming 'the truth that Jesus revealed.' The island of Patmos was one of several used by the Romans for banishment. The amenities would not be good but John had at least got away with his life. Perhaps he found deprivation of his people the most difficult thing to bear, and cut off from them, one Sunday, like any true pastor, he began to think with longing about his people and the dangers they were to face when the Domitian persecution got really under way. For some reason – perhaps it was brought on by thirst, for those islands were short of water – he fell into a trance, 'the Spirit took control', and he began to hear loud, insistent voices, like a trumpet, some of them saying things which were vaguely familiar, like this from Ezekiel. 'Then the Spirit lifted me up, and I heard behind me the voice of a great rushing, Blessed be the glory of the Lord from his place.' He looked round and what did he see?

The fanfare of the trumpet heralds the rising of the curtain on a scene of breathtaking splendour. It reveals 'a being who looked like a man', but a very special sort of man: transfigured, majestic, scintillating, shimmering, transplendent. Images from the Old Testament and apocalyptic writings crowd in on one another and with them John paints a portrait in light of all the attributes of God whose Word (for 'a sharp two-edged sword came out of his mouth') establishes truth and brings to nothing lies and vanity. Predictably, the sight of such an exalted being evokes *awe*. (Otto defined 'the holy' or 'the numinous' as the '*mysterium tremendum et fascinens*'. Kierkegaard labelled it 'dread'. Jacob found the overwhelming sense of God's nearness at Bethel 'dreadful'.) In the presence of this sublime and wonderful sight John, humbled, 'falls down at his feet like a dead man'. But he is quickly made to stand up again by the touch of Christ's 'right hand', for the whole point of the vision is not to overcome him, but to reassure him by showing Jesus resplendent with the attributes of God. He is told that he is in the presence of One who has tasted death, overcome it, and has now 'authority over death and the world of the dead'. But this picture of the exalted Lord must not diminish the notion that he is also with individual churches; for 'the secret meaning' – the unveiled mystery – 'of the seven stars' in his right hand is precisely that they are the location of his presence and the object of his concern. (For each church's 'candlestick' is the earthly counterpart of its 'star in the firmament' and its 'spirit in front of the throne'.) And John will be reiterating some aspects of the exalted vision when he comes to deal more specifically with the lowly churches. The emotional impact is such that we are reminded of Rilke's poem *The Archaic Torso of Apollo* . . . 'for there is no place that does not see you. You must, therefore, change your life.'

John is instructed to reassure Christians by passing on this vision of Jesus transfigured and divine. When he was transfigured on earth, to reassure his disciples who were entering a tough period Jesus told them to be quiet about what they had seen (Mark 9:1–9). But now the incognito is unnecessary, for his Godhead has been unveiled and his work is accomplished.

Whether 'the things you see, both the things that are now, and the things that will happen afterwards' refer respectively to the vision, the condition of the churches, and the Second Coming, or refer to the whole vision, seems not to matter very much. Neither does the question whether 'the angels' denote local church leaders or the heavenly sign of churches on the 'too, too sullied earth'.

The Message to Ephesus 2:1–7. Metropolitan Christianity

There are several reasons why John could have chosen Ephesus to head the list. (a) It was a pretty typical Pauline church. Moreover, Paul, who had spent three years amongst its members and left them amidst touching scenes (Acts 20:17–38), had already warned them, with tears in his eyes, that they were in for a time of troubles. 'I know that after I leave, fierce wolves will come among you, and they will not spare the flock.' (b) Ephesus was the principal city of Asia Minor. It was wealthy and cosmopolitan. Trade passed through it by land and water. It bustled with commercial life, but it also had the pomp and ceremony of an assize town. It was the home of the All-Ionian Games and prosperous citizens fell over themselves to become sponsors. The people tended to be snobbish about their political status for, though they had not home rule, they had been granted a measure of independence with a democratically-elected town council and a town-clerk of sorts. Ephesus could also boast one of the seven wonders of the ancient world: the Temple of Diana (or Artemis), the great mother. The vast, colonnaded court, resplendent with semi-precious jewels, was a sight for all to see. In its centre was the altar and, hidden behind a curtain, the ancient image of Diana, repellent and forbidding, her belly sprouting breasts in every direction like a gigantic loganberry, her hand grasping club and trident. Little wonder that this man-devouring monster was served by eunuchs and priestesses, full men keeping out of her way. The enclosure behind the altar acted as a strong-room where the rich could deposit their valuables when danger threatened but, paradoxically, any rogue or vagabond within a hundred yards of the altar could claim sanctuary. But, by the time of *Revelation*, Diana had had to move over to make room for intruders – the goddess Roma and the divine Julius, whose dignified worship contrasted starkly with the raucous 'muzak' and the lascivious dancing which accompanied the shout, 'Great is Diana, goddess of the Ephesians'. The makers of silver souvenirs did a roaring trade; but there was some friction when Christianity arrived because, if Diana and Roma were both ousted and supplanted by Jesus, the silversmiths would be out of a job and, to deal with the problem, a union meeting had to be called in the local Palace of Varieties (Acts 19: 21–41). So Ephesus – Westminster Abbey, Bank of England, Old Bailey, Guildhall, Wembley Stadium, Stock Exchange and Pop Festival rolled into one – was a fairly seductive and disagreeable place; so much so that it was said that her best-known son, the philosopher Heraclitus, never smiled!

(c) But perhaps John saw that the life of such a metropolis was going to be the milieu of the young church's testing, for it had taken root in cities 'in the cracks of a crumbling society', and the temptation to apostasy was always present. Thus the need to hold fast was imperative. It looks as though John's advice prevailed for, a score of years later, St Ignatius was praising the Christians' good deeds and harmonious love and the way they had stuck together under their pastor.

Trials had come all right. But, under the scrutiny of the divine presence, 'the one who walks among the candlesticks and holds the seven stars in his right hand', they had been patient, worked hard, and suffered troubles. Living as many of us do, in communities where worship is open and tolerated, we find it hard to understand the cost of discipleship when, as Kierkegaard might have put it, there are no *aesthetic* reasons for it. Once it is *à la mode* Christianity loses its significance.

The Ephesians had made a good start. They had weeded out those who were spreading ideas which were not consonant with the apostolic faith. They had been discriminating, and had shown the door to the Nicolaitans, whoever they were; the word means 'consumers of people' – laity! They had shown patience which, as Simone Weil has taught, means something more than waiting for troubles to pass by; more positively it means 'waiting on God' – in an attitude of openness and disposability.

The weeding-out process had only been achieved with cost. Anyone who has attended a church or parish meeting on some matter of principle knows how easily divisive situations arise. There had been the separation of those who should be together and thus the threat: 'I will come to you and take your lampstand from its place'. For the Presence departs when well-intentioned people, zealous to find the right way depart from the ultimate way, which is love. The times demand unity and understanding. For some of them martyrdom may be called for. But those who recall the way in which Jesus faced evil without its striking any echoing chords in him, and how he transmuted it into good, will conquer. That is victory; and the spoils? 'The right to eat the fruit of the tree of life that grows in the Garden of God' – a promise of Eden restored.

The Message to Smyrna 2:8–11 The Church Destitute

The words 'died and lived again' had special meaning for the Christians at Smyrna. For their city had been destroyed and, under Alexander the Great, had been rebuilt. It became the pride of Asia, displaying wide boulevards and arcades, several sumptuous temples to pagan gods, a sports-ground and, as befitted a place which claimed to be the birthplace of Homer, a quite splendid theatre. Living amongst all this splendour, very much like a back-street mission hall in the vicinity of Princes Street, Edinburgh, or Park Avenue, New York, were the Christians. John told them: 'I know that you are poor (lit. 'destitute') – but really you are rich!'

There appear to have been two sources of their 'troubles' (lit. 'pressures') which John knew all about. They were under pressure from the imperial authorities to conform to the state religion. Smyrna was proud of its loyalty to Rome and thankful for the good things that the *Pax Romana* had brought it. It seemed only decent to do the right thing by sacrificing the occasional pinch of incense, collecting the certificate ('We, N and N, the representatives of the Emperor, have seen you sacrificing') and then toddling round to the temple of their choice. But this the Christians were not prepared to do: the title 'Lord' was reserved for Jesus only. In fact 'Jesus is Lord' was the first credal confession.

They might indeed have got away with it, even in this centre of emperor worship, if there had not been present there a particularly nasty Jewish community who, perhaps jealous of the Christians' success amongst 'the god-fearers' – a group of pagan 'seekers' the Jews traditionally regarded as their proselytizing patch – were at pains to lay evidence against the Christians. Their hatred for Christians was unabated and when, some years later, dear old Polycarp, the bishop of Smyrna, was martyred at the stake at the age of eighty-six the Jews, even though it was the Sabbath, ran for wood to feed the flames. It stands to reason that the spoiling and vandalizing of Christian property by this 'group that belongs to Satan' would make for destitution.

John regards the persecutors as pseudo-Jews, and the

Christians as the true Israel, because they have been faithful to Jesus, in whose life and obedience unto death the Chosen People was reduced to one man. That is the richness they must hang on to. Some will die in the ensuing troubles. They will get the victor's crown which, in Smyrna, was a mark of high esteem and prestige and, though their bodies will be consumed, their spirits will be intact, and they will not have to succumb to the 'second death', (20:6; Matthew 10:28) which meant total annihilation. Others will go to prison for a short time. They will be called upon to witness by dying daily a hundred little deaths in a situation where, as Thoreau put it in *Walden*, men are compelled to 'lead lives of quiet desperation'.

> Christ leads me through no darker room
> Than he went through before;
> He that into God's kingdom comes
> Must enter by this door.
>
> Richard Baxter

The Message to Pergamum 2:12–17.
The Church amid Swords and Serpents

In Pergamum, 'Asia's foremost city' according to Pliny, and its administrative capital, there could be three contenders for the place 'where Satan has his throne'.

(a) There was a hill where Greek temples proliferated, for Pergamum had prided itself on being the last outpost of the old Greek Empire. Amongst these were temples to Athene, and an altar to Zeus which exists to this day. All day long the temples belched smoke from numberless sacrifices, and it lay like a pall over the city. But by John's time the Olympian gods, through their too-human excesses, were seen to have feet of clay, and their claims can hardly have been called diabolic.

(b) But Pergamum was also a centre of Asclepianism. Asclepius was a god of healing. Sanatoria were attached to the temples where the sick were laid in the hope that one of the sacred snakes would touch and heal them. (The serpent was Asclepius' symbol, and it is still contained in the insignia of the British Medical Association.) Indeed, the cult was so widespread in the empire that, with its insistence on healing, it paved the way for Christianity. John could be sensitive about it on two scores: worshippers tended to call Asclepius 'saviour', the predominant title of Jesus; and the serpent, in John's book, stood for the personification of evil. 'He is that old serpent, named the Devil, or Satan, that deceived the whole world' (12:9).

(c) However, by far the likeliest contender was emperor-worship which was extremely strong, and to which the city had an almost sycophantic leaning, proud to be called 'temple-sweepers'. A senatorial proconsul was resident there and his sign was the sword. The letter begins with 'the one who has the sharp two-edged sword', and it is therefore probable that John sees enthroned totalitarian power as the real threat, the real Satan, and it is his duty to remind the Christians that they are the citizens of another kingdom, the Kingdom of God who constitutes justice in his Word, Jesus Christ, and thus they must allow no other absolute claims to sovereignty. This made it perilous to be a Christian in Pergamum, and already one of their number, of whom we know nothing else, had been martyred, though it could just as easily have been by popular violence as the proper process of law.

Even so, John has to raise a couple of questions of social ethics. It was a problem that Paul had had to face at Corinth: should Christians eat meat sacrificed to idols? (cf. 1 Corinthians, Chapters 8 and 10.) It was really the so-called 'sin of Balaam', who made an effort to mix the pure life of Israel with the paganism which surrounded him (Numbers 23:1–2; 31:16). Superficially the issue seems trivial. Only a small part of the sacrificial animal was burned, the priest took his cut, and the worshipper was left with the rest. He was free to invite his friends round to a party, often at the temple, much in the same way as people today might invite guests to a club. But John did not want his people to compromise with the ruling class or cult. Following the tradition of the prophets, he realized that liberal views lead to licence, licence to laxity, and laxity to 'committing immorality', a phrase commonly used to describe getting mixed up with idolatry, though it could be taken in its literal sense, for the pagan temples in some cases kept prostitutes.

Those who take the risk of making an uncompromising stance with the values of this world are offered two extraordinary rewards: 'some of the hidden Manna' and 'a white stone, on which a new name is written'. There was a legend amongst the Jews that, when Jerusalem had fallen to the Babylonians in 586 BC, Jeremiah managed to hide the Ark of the Covenant in a cave. Among other things it contained a golden bowl of manna which would eventually be produced at the Messianic Banquet. Thus, those who refused the meat of idols would be fed on 'angels' food'. The meaning of the 'white stone' is less obvious. Stones were used in the ancient world for many purposes: for elections – if you got a white stone you were 'in'; as entrance tickets to circuses and banquets, like the metal tokens used at 'Wee Free' Church of Scotland communion services to this day; or as magic charms and amulets carrying an occult name. All these could be significant but no doubt 'a new name . . . which no one knows' is that of Christ who, whilst not shielding his followers from persecution will, if they remain faithful by living dangerously in not compromising with the standards of their neighbours, find themselves at the Messianic Feast. But John's exclusiveness raises enormous practical problems, and was not entirely shared by either Paul or, for that matter, by Jesus.

The Message to Thyatira 2:18–29.
The Church and Big Business

There were troubles at Thyatira, too, but this time they centred on 'that woman Jezebel, who calls herself a messenger of God'. Who was she? It would be tempting to say that she was the bishop's wife, and the little Greek word *sou* which appears in some manuscripts would make her that, presuming, of course, that 'the angel' refers to the bishop. Or could she have been Lydia from Thyatira? – who was a dealer in purple and who was baptized by Paul whilst she was on a business trip to Philippi (Acts 16:11–15) and who discovered, when she returned to base, that her new-found faith had cut her profit margins. The suggestion is fanciful, but the problem certainly was real. For Thyatira, though dismissed by Pliny as insignificant, thrived on the cloth-dyeing industry, was the HQ of the Purple Cloth Dyers' Federation, and a manufactory of the expensive purple dye. Membership of a craft guild was the *sine qua non* of getting on in business. But these were not concerned simply with rates and hours. There was the social and club life as well: feasting, sacrificing, and carousing – the 'old-boy network' and all that. Technically, of course, it was, once again, the question of meat sacrificed to idols. But the circular despatched to the churches after the Council of Jerusalem was absolutely unequivocal (Acts 15:20). To be a Christian virtually meant withdrawal from the mainstream of commercial life. How then were Christians to make a living? John, alas, offers them no advice but as he thought that there was not much time left, sound investment policies must have seemed irrelevant.

It does look as though what he feared most was that the purity of the apostolic faith would be contaminated. The allusion to Jezebel makes that clear. For she wanted to corrupt the pure worship of Jehovah by the introduction of the pagan Baal (2 Kings 9:22). This infuriated Elijah and, in a dramatic encounter on top of Mount Carmel, he had to call upon the people to choose (1 Kings 18). The present time called for similar decisiveness; it was no time for 'halting between two opinions'.

It also looks as though the danger came from within the Church, and that the woman, whoever she was, was trying to seduce Christians into playing with the deep secrets of Satan, tasting the experience of sin the more to understand and appreciate the liberation of redemption. But the Church was not without its resources for dealing with her. John said, 'I know your love,' ('*agape*', a distinctive Christian idea where love is rooted in the intention of the will, not in the vagaries of emotion) 'your faithfulness, your service, and your patience. I know that you are doing more now than you did at first.' There was growth in spirituality but the Son of God whose eyes blaze like fire (their coinage carried an image of Apollo, the sun-god with a halo of rays) 'knows men's thoughts and wishes' (lit. 'searches the heart and kidneys', regarded as the organs of thought and feeling respectively) so there was no room for complacency. Those who follow Jezebel will share her particularly nasty fate; and those 'who continue to do what I want until the very end' (lit. 'endure') will receive (a) 'authority over the nations, to rule them with an iron rod and to break them to pieces like clay pots', clearly a reference to the messianic hope in Psalm 2:8–9, attempts to soften which by some commentators are quite unconvincing; and (b) 'the morning star', which is clearly a reference to the resurrection glory of Christ who, in 22:16, is called 'the morning star'. Metamorphosis as a reward for virtue was a part of Greek mythology as well as Jewish apocalyptic writing.

The Message to Sardis 3:1–6. Nominal Christianity

Sardis, like Bradford, England, was a place 'where brass spoke'. For money had first been minted there and, with a prosperous sheep-rearing area at its hinterland, it had quickly become a textile centre. The clothing-trade had made it rich, and with it had come the gaudy things that follow commercial opulence: night-clubs (Herodotus had said 'they strum the guitar and sell by retail'), licentiousness, and loose-living. Sardis was also well in with Rome and when, in AD 17, the city was hit by an earthquake, the emperor remitted five years' taxes in order to pay for the rebuilding. There was one point, however, on which they were very sensitive. As one side of the city projected from sheer rock-face they had thought themselves to be impregnable. But twice the rock wall had been scaled at night, by both the Persians and the Greeks. So the words 'if you do not wake up, I will come upon you like a thief, and you will not even know the hour when I come' must have cut fairly near to the bone. They were too self-satisfied. There was no danger of being hauled before the Romans, ostracsized by the Jews, or of internal divisions. They merged easily into the cosy life of a community which had never had it so good. But they had the kiss of death on them, more through internal softness than outside pressure. They must 'watch' (cf. Matthew 24:36–44) and brace their spiritual muscles. They must 'strengthen (lit. 'fix') what you still have, before it dies completely'. Those who comply will be seen in the white robes of (inner) purity, joy, and conquest; and, since defaulting citizens in Sardis could have their names struck off the town register, their names will be kept on the 'book of the living' in the New Jerusalem; and in time of judgement the Lord himself will 'declare openly that they belong to me'. So Sardis is not without hope. 'They may discover new life.' They had that life at the beginning. Now 'the immeasurable privilege of their intimacy with him is only equalled by the peril of a half-hearted service given in return' (Caird).

The Message to Philadelphia 3:7–13.
The Church that Kept Faith

It would be agreeable to think that Philadelphia (which means 'brotherly love') got its name from the church there. It certainly merited such an honour because, with Smyrna, it is one of two churches against which John has nothing. It was a weak church ('I know that you have a little power' (lit. no 'dynamic')) but it looks as though their very weakness was a strength because there is no evidence that the cult of Dionysius, the god of drink and revelling, held any attraction for them. But three other aspects of the city's life suggest the theme of the letter: doors of opportunity, ultimate security, new names in a new city.

Uniquely, the letter does not begin with any of the appellations of Christ from chapter 1. Instead it uses 'the one who is holy and true', a description which carries the overtones of reliability, loyalty, and steadfastness. It was he who would provide the dynamic for this pitifully weak church to undertake an important task. Philadelphia had been planned as a centre for the spreading eastward of Greek culture and language, and it was known as the Gateway to the East. Similarly there was a 'door of opportunity' being opened for the church to evangelize the Jews, 'that group that belongs to Satan'. He who holds 'the key that belonged to David' (Isaiah 22:22) 'holds the key to earthly opportunity as well as to heavenly glory' (Caird) and will have the power to admit or exclude from the Holy City.

Verse 9 is a clear harking-back to the hope that all

pagan nations would come to acknowledge the Jews (Isaiah 60:14) but John gives it a painful twist for the Jews by telling the Christians that it is they, not the Jews, who are 'the vines of the Lord's own planting', the true Israel. 'They will all know that I love you.'

The country round Philadelphia was subject to earthquakes, and the people had frequently to take to the fields and the open country when tremors were felt. John promises them a security which means that they will never have to leave it again. But this safety is found only in the city not made with hands, and the price of an 'ultimate security' there and then is constancy now 'in the hour of temptation' which is already upon them. 'Because you have kept my order to be patient, I will also keep you safe from the time of trouble which is coming upon the whole world, to test all the people on earth.' The Jews' Golden Age was not, like that of the Greeks, in the past, but in the future. In between their paradisaical beginning and the looked-for Day of the Lord there would be the Judgement, when the wheat would be sifted from the chaff. Those who remained true during that 'crisis' would win the reward of their fidelity. The Christian lives *always* under the same crisis.

The earthquake of AD 17 levelled Philadelphia as well as Sardis. It was rebuilt, again with help from the Emperor, and the new city was given a new name (Neocaesarea) which for some reason did not stick. But citizens of the new town who had achieved distinction had their names carved on pillars in the temple. Christians who were faithful would be rewarded by seeing their names not only in the Lamb's book of Life, but on one of the Temple pillars in the New Jerusalem. (There *was* no temple there; but consistency is not one of John's strong points!) They will also be given a 'new name'. Names, to the Asians, were virtually tangible things. Give a man your name and you virtually gave him a share in your life. You handed over a control and you were careful, therefore, to whom you gave your name. Remember 'wrestling Jacob' (Genesis 32). To receive the 'new name' of Christ is, thus, to participate in his life. 'In the temple built of souls, the Christian person is, of course, an essential support. And this victorious person is to bear the signature of God, the signature of the city of God amongst men, and the signature of the living Christ. He is to bear the seal of the victory of God in history' (L. H. Hough).

The Message to Laodicea 3:14–22. Tepid Christianity

We now come to the only one of the seven churches to add an adjective to the English language, and a pretty discreditable one at that: 'Laodicean – lukewarm . . . esp. in politics or religion, 1633' (Shorter Oxford Dictionary). It was this half-hearted religion which made John sick. For, in his view, a religion without enthusiasm was not a religion at all; nor is it, for 'enthusiasm' means 'God-filled'.

Laodicea was to Asia what Zurich is to Europe. It was of no military importance whatever, but its geographical situation had made for rapid commercial growth. It was a banking centre, though whether this was developed by the abnormally large Jewish community there we do not know. In any event it was rich, and proud of it; so rich in fact that when imperial help was offered for rebuilding after an earthquake in AD 60 it was politely declined and the rebuilding was funded by the wealthy citizens.

It was also the home of a flourishing textile industry. The flocks of sheep grazing on the surrounding hills produced a shiny, fine, black wool which was turned into coats which were much sought after by would-be notables looking for status symbols. There was a medical school there which had patented an eye-salve known as 'Phrygian powder'. A walk down *Bahnhofstrasse* in Zurich shows some of the things which John saw as dangerous seductions for the church at Laodicea: palpable wealth, banking 'gnomes', a virile textile trade, and a pharmaceutical industry offering specific remedies against every ailment and tonics for the indefinite prolongation of this mortal life. There was no wonder that a church in the midst of such a very wealthy community had settled for the sort of religion which did not disturb middle-class respectability. It was such a blatant compromise with the world that made John remark that in everything that mattered they were 'poor, naked and blind'. 'All right', he says to them in effect, 'rich and well-off you may think yourselves; but my advice is to get gold, not from the banks, but the pure gold (lit. 'fire-tested') which only costly obedience can produce; throw away those expensive black coats, they only hide your shame. Buy also white clothing – symbol of purity – to dress yourselves. Forget about those quack remedies. A simple bread-poultice will help you to improve your spiritual vision.' John had no time for their lukewarmness. He wanted them to be hot (lit. 'at boiling point', Greek *zestos*).

But who or what is to be the source of such renewal? – 'the Amen, the faithful and true witness, who is the origin of all that God has created.' He is 'the amen' – the 'let it be so' – because he is the man who is true to type, the man who is what he says. 'For us fights the proper man' (Luther). The strength of 'the amen' will revitalize them and help them find their true vocation amidst the fading riches of this world. For 'the amen' is not just the highest to which a man has aspired. He is the origin of all that God created, as Paul has made clear in Colossians. 'Christ is the visible likeness of the invisible God. He is the firstborn son, superior to all created things. For by him God created everything in heaven and on earth, the seen and the unseen things, including spiritual powers, lords, rulers, and authorities. God created the whole universe through him and for him. He existed before all things, and in union with him all things have their proper place' (Colossians 1:15–17). It is only in union with such a potent power, only if they manifest such a connection, that middle-class churches can be said to have found their 'proper place'.

A church immured in compromise at every point was a painful prospect for John, but he did not think that even it was beyond redemption. There was hope for it. But there was a price to be paid. 'I reprove and punish all whom I love.' With chastening they may, even still, be able to witness to 'the amen' in a city which has got its values upside down. 'The task of the Christian is always to swim against the tide' (Emil Brunner). Even now Christ is waiting at the door and knocking. All they have to do is to open. Whether this is a clear reference to the Second Coming or, like Holman Hunt's famous picture, *The Light of the World*, a tugging at the heart-strings of the individual believer, the urgency is the same. And so is the promise. Christ will be the guest at supper which, for them, was the main meal of the day. There he will be 're-presented' (the Eucharistic allusions are clear) to those who are victorious, to those who have won the victory by refusing to compromise, even though it entails martyrdom, or by any kind of true witness. 'I have been victorious.' The promise is that the faithful will reign with Jesus. But Jesus 'reigns from the tree'. Victory for the Christian lies in the same direction as that of his Lord, 'whom to serve is to reign'.

And so, with a strong affirmation of the 'nonsense of neutrality' the Letter to the Seven Churches ends. It is a hard and uncompromising letter, saying in effect that the alternatives are enthusiasm or nothing. It raises disturbing questions about the relevance of impossible ethical ideals in an industrialized, pluriform society such as ours. It raises also the distinction made by Emil Brunner between the Church as a 'community of culture' and the Church as 'a community of faith'. In the church at the grass roots these are inextricably mixed up. St Augustine saw both a City of Man and a City of God, and there is perhaps no answer to the question, 'To what degree is the first an incubus on the second?' One principle at least is clear: 'the very phrase "lukewarm Christian" is a contradiction in terms; for a lukewarm Christian has no claim to be a Christian at all' (Barclay).

Worship in Heaven Chapters 4 and 5.
The Almighty, The Lamb, and the Scroll

Having had a look at some of 'the things that are' on the earth the time has come to have a look at 'the things that are' in heaven. Hitherto, the symbols have been relatively straightforward and their meaning relatively plain. From here onwards they will become more difficult and complex. The mind will boggle at the task of trying to put together some of the creatures from the descriptions given, and when it does so, though their symbolic meaning may be clear, their appearance may be grotesque. Take comfort, for in *The Face of the Deep* Christina Rossetti had the same difficulty.

'Much of this awful Apocalypse opens to my apprehension rather a series of aspects than any one defined and certified object. It summons me to watch and pray and give thanks; it urges me to climb heavenward. Its threads doubtless consist unbroken; but my clue is at the best woven of broken lights and shadows, here a little and there a little. As when years ago I abode some while within sight of a massive sea rock, I used to see it put on different appearances; it seemed to float baseless in air, its summit vanished in cloud, it displayed upon its surface varied markings, it passed from view altogether in a mist, it fronted me distinct and solid far into the luminous summer night, still appearing many and various while all the time I knew it to be one and the same – so now this Apocalypse I know to be one congruous, harmonious whole, yet can I read it only as it were in disjointed portions, some to myself inexplicable, some not unmistakably defined; all nevertheless, please God, profitable to me for doctrine, for reproof, for correction, for instruction in righteousness.' (Christina Rossetti, *The Face of the Deep*, pp. 174–5.)

This is finely put and speaks for us all. Reading *Revelation* is like 'spiralling' a mountain. For much of the time the summit is lost to view, but every now and then it reappears, a few hundred feet nearer, and assures us that it is still there, and the climb will be worth its while. We are in an infinitely better position to understand the book than Christina Rossetti. Inter-testamentary scholarship has been enormous and instructive. We know more than Christina Rossetti about the sources of the apocalyptic symbolism with which John's mind was brimming over. Yet we still have to trust that the 'thread consists unbroken' and be content 'with broken lights and shadows'.

If I had been an illuminator working on a vellum manuscript of *Revelation* in one of the medieval scriptoria, I know what pictures I would have chosen to work into the initial letters of the first word in chapters 4 and 5. For chapter 4 I should have painted the throne of the Almighty and 'all round the throne . . . a rainbow the colour of an emerald', for the rainbow was the sign of the covenant of God's mercy. Into the initial of chapter 5 I should have worked the *Lamb and Scroll*, which is the symbol not only *of* victory but of its *means*: not brute force, sultanic power, but defenceless and suffering love. Keep these two brightly-coloured pictures at the back of your mind during everything that follows. For they are two of the three vital symbols in the next part of the vision.

John now saw a door in heaven open and heard a loud voice saying, 'Come up here, and I will show you what must happen after this.' Doubtless when he felt the trance of the Spirit coming over him, and realized his destination, he was filled with apprehension and excitement for 'up here' meant the Central Operations Room for the whole universe. What did he expect to see? Believing, as he did, that the Almighty was about to intervene dramatically in the sinful affairs of men, he could have been disappointed not to see scenes of frenzied martial preparation. But he found nothing of the sort. It was business as usual. The Central Operations Room was engaged in the *central act* of religion. 'The first or central act of religion is *adoration*, sense of God, his otherness, though nearness, his distinction from all finite beings, though not separateness – aloofness – from them.' (von Hügel, *Selected Letters*, p. 261.)

The first part, then, of the vision of heaven, is devoted to God Almighty. No doubt it came as a tonic to those persecuted Christians when they saw the splendour and majesty and power of God projected by those scintillating images of his Presence and the radiance surrounding his throne. The precise meaning of some of the details is anybody's guess, and it would be easy to fill the page with references and footnotes. Who were 'the twenty-four elders'? Angels? (cf. Hanson and Preston). Not very likely as they are separately mentioned in 5:11. And why twenty-four – the twelve apostles plus the twelve patriarchs? As they wear white robes (the sign of purity) and keep doffing and donning their golden crowns (the sign of victory) they could be a court of martyrs. 'Flashes of lightning, sounds, and peals of thunder', which crop up again later, were often associated with divine activity (Exodus 19:16). The 'lighted torches burning before the throne' refer back to 1:4, forward to 5:6, and derive from Zechariah 4:2. 'The sea of glass, clear as crystal' is something of a puzzle. Dr Caird thinks it is the symbol of a 'bad thing', for the sea is that which separates God from his people, as it separated John from his. He mentions that in the New World there 'is no more sea'. Certainly the Bible-men did not like the sea. It was the home of their monster, Leviathan, and when they wanted to indicate God's power they were inclined to show his mastery over it. 'Here shall your proud waves be stayed.' 'Can you (Job) catch Leviathan on a hook?' But the sea around Patmos does shimmer with mirror-like serenity, and the words may mean the unruffled tranquillity of heaven.

The 'living creatures' derive from Ezekiel 1 and represent the *cherubim*, though on the way they have picked up some of the equipment of the *seraphim* from Isaiah's vision of God exalted in chapter 6. The *cherubim* were not like chubby infants advertising baby soap but agents of God's power. In heaven they never stop singing. Now, joined by the elders, they give voice to two songs, probably examples of early congregational praise. 'You are worthy' was a form of address used with emperors. 'Glory' carries with it the sense of 'esteem' as well as that of splendour. Thus the first hymn lauds the otherness (holiness, separateness) of God, and the second his goodness shown in his providence; all creation was by his will given 'existence and life'. (The thought of John 1:1–4, though not the Gospel, for it was not written, where the Word is shown as the agent of *Creation*, makes a transition to the next part of the vision where the Word is shown as the agent of *Redemption*.)

At this stage it would be a good idea for the reader, if he has not already done so, to look at Ezekiel 1:1–3:3, because this contains much of the imagery lying behind the visions so far, and clearly holds the antecedent of the third important symbol, '[the scroll] covered with writing on both sides, and . . . sealed with seven seals'. Here again God is having trouble with rebellious nations and the scroll carries the battle plan for the overthrow and subjugation of those who serve Satan. That is why John, who looks forward so ardently to the final victory of God, breaks into tears, overcome with emotion that though the design for victory has been worked out, there is nobody worthy to be privy to it or carry it out. But one of the elders knows better. 'Don't cry. Look! The Lion from Judah's tribe, the great descendant of David, has won the victory and can break the seven seals and open the scroll.' It is rather a pity that Stephanus, who versified the New Testament, much of it being done on a horse, did not run this verse on for a few words, for it would have made one of the most dramatic transformation scenes in the whole of the Bible. 'Then I saw a Lamb standing in the centre of the throne.'

Something of the quite staggering effect this transformation of images must have had on the original readers may be experienced in the last lines of W. B. Yeats' 'The Second Coming'.

Turning and turning in the widening gyre
The falcon cannot hear the falconer;
Things fall apart; the centre cannot hold;
Mere anarchy is loosed upon the world,
The blood-dimmed tide is loosed, and everywhere
The ceremony of innocence is drowned;
The best lack all conviction, while the worst
Are full of passionate intensity.
Surely some revelation is at hand;
Surely the Second Coming is at hand.
The Second Coming! Hardly are those words out
When a vast image out of *Spiritus Mundi*
Troubles my sight; somewhere in sands of the desert
A shape with lion body and the head of a man,
A gaze blank and pitiless as the sun,
Is moving its slow thighs, while all about it
Reel shadows of the indignant desert birds.
The darkness drops again; but now I know
That twenty centuries of stony sleep
Were vexed to nightmare by a rocking cradle,
And what rough beast, its hour come round at last,
Slouches towards Bethlehem to be born.[1]

The lamb, which 'appeared to have been killed' in the heart of God's presence, marks the critical and fundamental shift in messianic expectation. The hope of a Messiah who was a lion, yes, that was all right, for a lion represented coercive power, and the Jewish commentaries on Isaiah 53, which colours Christian understanding of the mission of Jesus, went out of their way to state that the lamb 'led to the slaughter' was of no messianic significance. But here is 'the lamb', grotesquely drawn with seven horns (power), seven eyes (omniscience), and all-sufficient (seven). 'The Lamb . . . took the scroll from the right hand (the place of power) of the one who sat on the throne.' He is about to put into effect what the scroll contains.

> 'Jesus did not change the divine plan; he unfolded its eternal and unchangeable nature by his obedience even unto the death of the cross.' (Hanson & Preston)

No wonder there was praise in heaven, accompanied by incense and harps: 'thousands and millions of [angels] . . . and . . . every creature in heaven, on earth, and in the world below, and every creature in the sea – all creatures in the whole universe' join in. All things join in the hymn celebrating the victory and divinity of Jesus – in the whole New Testament never more than here. As Evelyn Underhill writes:

> 1. (W. B. Yeats, *Collected Poems*, 1933, Macmillan.)
> 'We already see a developed worship of the whole company of the faithful focused upon the altar. The Object of worship is both transcendent and redemptive; the Eternal and Omnipotent God . . . the Lamb that was slain on the altar of humanity, the self-given sacrament of Divine Love. The *Sanctus* . . . is already heard as the song of the whole created order . . . The Eucharistic and redemptive references of this sublime picture, its Christocentric characters, are clear.' (*Worship*, Fontana, p. 100)

There is also here a hint that just as the Passover Lamb's blood protected the first-born of the Israelites from the plague of death, 'the lamb of God who takes away the sins of the world' will protect the faithful from the wrath to come.

And so, with these splendid affirmations of God's almighty goodness and mercy ringing in his ears, the reader can look with confidence on the horrors about to be let loose.

The Seals 6:1–8. The Four Horsemen

We are not told how the breaking of one seal on a scroll allows it to be opened, but the Lamb breaks a seal and a 'living creature' says 'Come!' It is tempting to guess at what John expected to be in the scroll during the seconds between the 'living creature' – one of God's agents – giving the order, and the first horse appearing. Certainly both his own experience and his own reading would have conditioned him to expect 'a time of troubles'. Daniel (12:1) had foretold 'a time of troubles, such as there never was since there was a nation' and John had enough material to document the notion from three sources:

a) His own experience: virtually all his adult life had been spent contemplating catastrophe of one sort or another – earthquakes, the Neronian persecution, the sack of Jerusalem, the anarchy followng Nero's suicide, famine, and such a violent eruption of Vesuvius that men expected the end of the world.

b) The teaching of prophecy: Isaiah, Joel, Hosea, Amos, had a marvellous readiness of mind to conjure up Doomsday, and even suggested that it would be worse than they could imagine.

c) The express teaching of the Law: Leviticus 26 gives a vivid picture of what happens if God's precepts are disobeyed – 'if ye reject my commandments . . . I will appoint terror over you' (v. 15f).

And it was terror the horsemen brought in their train. Inspired by Zechariah 1:8–11 and 6:1–8 – where, with their chariots, they were a kind of celestial mobile patrol, reporting back on conditions amongst men, their colours signifying different sectors – they arrive, each at the behest of a 'living creature', with *a woe.*

a) 'There was a white horse. Its rider held a bow, and he was given a crown. He went out as a conqueror to conquer.' This is no doubt an allusion to invasion, possibly the Parthians, who shot a good arrow and had humiliated a Roman army some thirty years earlier.

b) 'Another horse came out, a red one. Its rider was given the power to bring war on the earth, that men should kill each other' – civil war and internal strife.

c) 'A black horse. Its rider held a pair of scales in his

hand.' A voice said, 'A quart of wheat for a whole day's wages, and three quarts of barley for a whole day's wages' – barely subsistence living, inflation, and rationing. Nobody knows the meaning of the second part of the verse.

d) 'A pale (lit. 'sickly') coloured horse. Its rider was named Death, and Hades followed close behind.' The two are also together in 1:18 and 20:13–14. They bring sickness, pestilence, and death, the corollaries of strife.

These *woes* and those that follow add up to 'the wrath of the Lamb' (6:16) and it is proper to ask whether, and in what way, John envisaged the Lamb to have caused them. I am not as convinced as other commentators that John was above tingeing the deity with a touch of revenge, but I have already hinted at the grounds on which the Lamb can be exonerated, for it is scarcely credible that John, even with his penchant for inconsistency, would root affliction in the will of the Crucified.

These disasters are man-made. There is no natural calamity amongst them. They result from injustice and man's failure to achieve true community. They are thus the result of not taking God's law seriously. God wills community, which is the end of love. Leviticus spelt out the consequences of ignoring the precepts. Ignore physical laws, like stepping off a cliff, and disaster follows; neglect moral laws and disaster ensues just as surely. The situation in the world which John looked upon, and which he is going to paint in vivid hues, is the consequence of infringing the will of God. The *woes* are therefore the result of not taking seriously his command to achieve community and justice. He does not will them; but as long as man is a free agent he allows them. It was this that St Paul saw as the guilt of mankind: 'God's wrath . . . coming down from heaven upon all the sin and evil of men whose evil ways prevent the truth from being known' (Romans 1:18). C. H. Dodd's fine commentary on this verse has shown that though Paul speaks of the *wrath of God* on several occasions he clearly never makes God the subject of the verb 'to be angry'. But then Paul was able to use a theological concept to describe a moral law! By the same token the Lamb did not *will* the woes.

The Seals 6:9–11. The Impatient Martyrs

The breaking of the fifth seal may reflect some of John's own doubts and uncertainties, for it shows the martyrs underneath the heavenly altar crying out, 'How long will it be until you judge the people of earth and punish them for killing us?' The answer given is not altogether satisfactory, probably because they have asked the question in a way which smacks of a desire for revenge and retribution. But they had a fair point. For if there was to be no final triumph of good over evil then their sacrifice was in vain. Each of them is then given a white robe, symbolizing victory and light, and maybe signifying the resurrection body with a translucence that is tantamount to spiritual energy. If this is so, John's conception of a resurrection body resembles that set out by Paul in 1 Corinthians 15, where it is made clear that in his view our resurrection bodies are indissolubly linked with what we do with our mortal bodies and only grow to the degree 'that we carry in our mortal bodies the death of Jesus' in a life of continuous witness.

But these martyrs who have achieved their resurrection bodies – if that is what the white robe is intended to convey – are also counselled to be patient and wait until 'the total number was reached of their fellow servants and brothers who were to be killed.' This, in some respects, continues the previous notion. As Dr Caird has pointed out, it cannot mean that there was an 'only a few vacancies' notice outside heaven, or that the 'noble army of martyrs' had to be mustered into one company before the End was possible; but, just as the opening of the scroll depended on the obedience unto death of Jesus, so the End will come and God's purpose will be achieved by the continuous martyrdom of his followers.

When the sixth seal is broken a flood of natural disasters is let loose. It is reminiscent of 'The Little Apocalypse' in Mark 13 – as though the evil times spoken of by the prophets have been *brought to remembrance*, that is, 'actualized', not simply 'reminded of' (Isaiah 2:12–17; 34:2–4; Joel 2:28ff; Amos 4:1ff.) These earth-shaking happenings make everyone, irrespective of class, bolt for the open country in frenzied despair, hoping there to find cover from 'the eyes of the one who sits on the throne, and from the wrath of the Lamb'. This 'shaking of the foundations' prompted the author of Hebrews to write 'that the created things will be shaken and removed, so that the things that are not shaken will remain'. It was an awe-full day.

The 144,000 People of Israel 7:1-17. A Hopeful Interval

There is now an interval in the action whilst 'angels' restrain the destructive 'winds' until they have marked 'the servants of our God with a seal on their foreheads'. This is to protect them from harm when the action is resumed and all hell is let loose at the breaking of the seventh seal. There may be an allusion here to the marking of the righteous (Ezekiel 9:1–8) before the destruction of Jerusalem, and there are overtones of baptism which in the second century was known as the 'seal', and also, as noted above, the Passover. 'Twelve thousand' from each of the twelve tribes of Israel make 144,000, but the number must not be taken literally, and only metaphorically makes up the tally required by the impatient martyrs. It represents the complete Christian Church (v. 9). Caird makes a rather far-fetched suggestion that only the martyrs need this protection because only they are on active service, but the comment he makes provides an illuminating bridge to the next section. 'In John's vision of the heavenly council he heard a voice speak of the Lion of Judah and when he looked to see this lion he in fact saw a Lamb. So in thc present passage what John *hears* is the scriptural image of the army of Israel' – Dan is missing, because tradition had it that it would provide Antichrist – 'but what he sees is the Christian fact of the noble army of martyrs' (p. 96).

'They were from every race, tribe, nation, and language . . . dressed in white robes . . . They called out in a loud voice, "Our salvation comes from our God." ' To signify victory, their robes have been 'dazzlingly whitened' (the same word as in the story of the Transfiguration) in the blood of the Lamb. When Jesus spoke of baptism – 'I have a baptism to be baptized with' (Luke 12:50, Mark 10:38) – he meant the death of the cross. Transfiguration followed his realization of its necessity. The martyrs stand in the same tradition. They witness, but they sing that their 'salvation' (which here means victory) is a gift, and 'comes from our God'. He who has given the victory now becomes the ground of their bliss. 'Tell the miracle abroad! God makes himself so low that he himself becomes the pasture for his lambs' (Angelus Silesius).

The Seventh Seal 8:1–5 – The Trumpets 8:6 – 9:21. The Plagues

John was an apocalyptist in the great tradition. Only Cecil B. de Mille could have realized the vastness of his scenario. The Lamb breaks the Seventh Seal which is to herald the End. This is the big moment. The reader holds his breath – he braces himself for the worst. But nothing happens. Just pure silence. 'There was silence in heaven for about half an hour.' The continuous performance of heavenly worship is interrupted to allow an angel to offer 'the prayers of all God's people' on earth, giving them the sanction of heaven by 'censing' them on 'the gold altar that stands before the throne'. Their prayers – the intention of the Church – seem to be necessary to what follows, for the angel took a bowl full of 'fire from the altar and threw it on the earth'. Then – Bang! Cosmic consequences follow the opening of the seventh seal: thunder, earthquakes – signs that God is present.

An angel sounds a trumpet – a symbol about which many meanings cluster but is here clearly a summons to repentance. And it must be remembered in what ensues that, dire though the imagery is, the aim is repentance and not vengeance. Though nothing is done to minimize the gravity of sin and rebellion against God, or the fact that there are fates worse than physical death, there is great emphasis on God's patience and mercy. It is only because of their continued recalcitrance that pressure on the men of earth is progressively increased.

Firstly, there is a series of four plagues which aim at the partial destruction of natural resources – the 'one third' harking back to a notion that a third of the world's woes would come with the advent of the Messiah: agriculture, fishing, water and light are all affected, the hope no doubt being that, deprived of life's amenities, men would learn that they do not live by bread alone. But there is a clue to something else. Christians may take heart even though doom may be imminent on earth. There is an allusion to the impending fall of the new Babylon, which will be developed later (Jeremiah 51:25, 42; Isaiah 14:12–20, 'Heylel' denoting Babylon, and the new Egypt, both of which are Rome). There is therefore the hint of a new Exodus, to set the Church, the 'new Israel', free and this is confirmed when the sequence of trumpets is interrupted by the screech of 'an eagle that was flying high in the air' (lit. 'in mid-heaven'). For, when Israel arrived on the plain of Sinai, God told Moses, 'Ye have seen what I did unto the Egyptians, and how I bare you on eagles' wings, and brought you unto myself' (Exodus 19:4).

But the eagle brings cold comfort. (Some versions have 'carrion'.) He announces how 'horrible' it is going to be for the 'unsealed' worldly men – 'for all who live on earth' – when the rest of the trumpets blast off. So a fifth angel sounds. A falling (not fallen) star, that is a principality or power with its heavenly angel, is 'given' (everything happens by the Creator's consent) 'the key to the abyss'. This is not Sheol where the spirits of men may find temporary accommodation. It is the location of palpable evil, according to Enoch 'horrible and chaotic' and (v. 11) King Chaos 'the destroyer' rules there. Deprivation of the basics of living having proved to be of no avail, man's physical comfort is now attacked until he is brought to the point of despair, that 'sickness unto death'. The agent is a swarm of locusts pictured brilliantly and energetically and drawn from Joel 1:6–7 and 2:4–5. But this is not enough either. So another trumpet sounds. It announces a chilling and blood-curdling vision: sanctioned from on high, 'a voice coming from the corners of the gold altar', a couple of hundred million mounted troops incinerate, asphyxiate, and poison 'a third of all mankind'. Probably they were Parthians, whom the Romans frenetically feared, and who discharged their arrows fore and aft.

The survivors are left untouched and do not 'turn away from what they themselves had made'. Typical of Marcuse's 'one-dimensional man', they are materialist, and preoccupied with their own little goals and ends (idols). They want to go it alone. In their pride they think they can achieve their own destiny. Dependence on a creator, or on any value which transcends the immediate, is meaningless. Or they become the prisoner of sensual experience unrelated to care (immorality). Or they attach themselves to bogus quasi-religions (magic) which Spengler, in *The Decline of the West*, calls the 'second religiousness' which marks the end of an age.

The Angel and the Little Scroll 10:1–11

Any moment we may expect the Great Distress. But no, there is another pause. Just as there was an interval before the breaking of the seventh seal, so there is now an interval before the sounding of the last trumpet. We need some reassurance. So we are back on earth with the vision of a literally colossal angel filling the whole screen, straddling earth and sea, to mark the world-wide consequences of what is to follow.

> Stupendous form! the vast Colossus stood . . .
> Betwixt his brazen thighs in loose array
> Ten thousand streamers on the billows play.

He is almost godlike in his attributes: clouds, rainbow, radiant sun, the hallmarks of divinity. With legs 'like columns of fire', he will guide the Church through the wilderness and the darkness which persecution is to bring upon it. Seven thunders express the divine will, but John is told not to note what they contain – sufficient for Christians to know that the End will come without delay, their role set out in 'the open scroll' which John is handed, with instructions to eat it, hinting that though in his mouth it 'will be sweet as honey', when he has really digested its contents 'it will turn sour in your stomach.' It does exactly that. Glad that the Day is imminent John is pained when he realizes what must be gone through before everything is accomplished. Only a resplendent vision of the ultimate victory of God and the rightness of the Christian cause could give the churches the courage and dynamic to pay the price. Already what had happened under Nero was well known. Tacitus has left a grim picture: 'an immense multitude was convicted, not so much of firing the city, as of hatred against mankind.

Mockery of every kind was added to their deaths. Covered with the skins of beasts, they were torn by dogs and perished, or were nailed to crosses, or were doomed to the flames and burnt to serve as a nightly illumination at the emperor's wine festivals.' (Tacitus, *Annals* Book 15: 44.) If this was the consequence of swimming against the tide of pagan life – 'hatred of mankind' – no wonder John's stomach turned over. But this is the means of redemption that God has chosen to overcome man's recalcitrance and rebellion. And John has no alternative but to announce it to 'many nations, races, languages, and kings'. (Cf. Daniel 12 which is the basis of this chapter.)

The Two Witnesses 11:1–14

This is the second so-called 'intermezzo' vision. It holds the action in suspense, but it is vital to the primary purpose of *Revelation*, which is pastoral, and it is thus of capital importance for us. Space forbids recounting the critical battles which Bible-scholars have fought over it for a detailed exploration of the images it contains. Readers who know Bunyan's 'City of Destruction' and 'Vanity Fair' will find striking resemblances here. There are four main symbols: the Temple, the Two Witnesses, the Beast, and the Great City.

John is given a rule to measure the Temple. He knows that the Temple of the Jews had been in ruins for twenty years, and he has no desire to see it rebuilt. It is the other Temple, the one 'not made with hands', which is his concern here. The true Temple would never again be made of bricks and mortar. It now exists only in Christ's body, the Church. John's concern is to keep it inviolate. 'Measuring' in the Old Testament normally meant marking for destruction; but during the inter-testamentary period it came to mean the opposite. In Enoch the 'angels bring the measure of the righteous . . . for none shall be destroyed before the Lord of the spirits' (61:1–5) and it is in this sense that John uses it here. The Church of Christ will therefore survive the coming Great Distress. The gates of hell will not prevail against it. It will suffer, because the 'heathen' will 'trample on the Holy City for 42 months' – a conventional duration for persecution, dating from the length of time that the Syrian conqueror, Antiochus

Epiphanes, had his bust in the Temple in Jerusalem. But during this same period of 1260 days two 'witnesses' or prophets 'will proclaim God's message'.

The symbol of the witnesses is a good example of the way John's mind, steeped in allusion and imagery, works tradition into his own story. He begins with Zechariah (4:1–4) who was associated with the rebuilding of the Temple after the Exile. Two olive trees fed the lamps. These two 'sons of oil that stand before the Lord of the earth' were probably Joshua, the High Priest, and Zerubabbel, the Governor, the representatives of ecclesiastical and civil authority. They played a vital role in rebuilding the Temple. They suddenly become 'two lamps', which are symbols of the Church, the totality of which is found in the seven lamps. So the Church is to be the witness. More power to its prophecy springs from yet another symbolic transformation into Elijah, who shut up the sky (1 Kings 17:1) and Moses, who turned water into blood (Exodus 7:17), both of whom survived into all eternity. Into their prophetic role the Church must now enter, testifying – before Roman magistrates? – with 'fire . . . out of their mouths'.

'The beast that comes up out of the abyss will fight against them . . . and kill them' and 'their bodies will lie on the street of the great city.' Which city? The text says 'the great city, where their Lord was nailed to the cross. The symbolic name of that city is Sodom, or Egypt.' These names cluster together to give a city which is all cities and none. It is Metropolis – 'people from all nations' – a mythical city, the seat of despotic power, the home of the equally mythical Beast, the latest incarnation of which is Rome.

Because the two witnesses have 'brought so much suffering upon the people of earth' there is dancing in the streets when they are killed, and their bodies are left on view. The crowd, which trampled on the Holy City, have a carnival because they can now carry on the *dolce vita* without being disturbed. It was probably this prophetic criticism of the Roman way of life which caused civic authorities to accuse the Christians of 'hating humanity'.

Is it too fanciful to hear echoes of another beast, the one mentioned by Plato (Book VI of *The Republic*) who held that worshipping the Great Beast meant acting and legislating cynically, that is not from the standpoint of truth and justice, but with an eye on the value of the majority, and thus becoming the lackey of public opinion? Jeremiah had to complain about it in his day: 'a . . . horrible thing is come to pass . . . and my people love to have it so' (Jeremiah 5:30–31) Kierkegaard wrote, 'The crowd is the lie!' Simone Weil, throughout her work, saw the Great Beast as 'the collective'. 'The collective is the object of all idolatry, this it is which chains us to the earth.' 'The social order is irreducibly the prince of this world.' She saw the Great Beast not only in states (as distinct from countries) and even in the Roman Catholic Church. She also saw that the greatest threat to the modern world is its uprootedness (*déracinement*) from the world of transcendental values and qualities so that it has no 'yardstick' by which to judge its life. Opportunism and amenity then hold sway. Conformity to purely social virtue may, indeed, be a form of idolatry.

The rejoicing of the crowd is short-lived, however, for the prophet-witnesses are resurrected and assumed into heaven, a signal for more earthquakes which destroy one tenth of Metropolis and kill 7000 people. Those who remain on earth, for there is still time to repent, are terror-stricken and praise God, no doubt, that they have got away with their lives, for there is no sign that they are going to repent!

The Seventh Trumpet 11:15–19

So the second horror passes. We are told to expect a third. The screech of an eagle stirs the memory. The last trumpet sounds. It must surely be a call to arms for that final battle between good and evil for which Christians have so attentively listened. It must herald the big scene. And it does. But not the one we expect. The trumpet does not sound the alarm, but a fanfare. We come round a shoulder of the moutain and are allowed to see the summit. We are back in heaven again. There is a great shout: 'The power to rule over the world belongs now to our Lord and his Messiah, and he will rule for ever and ever.' Then this, the leitmotive of *Revelation*, is taken up in a hymn which celebrates the end of worldly rule (of

Satan epitomized by Rome) and its replacement by the rule (or kingdom) of God in Jesus Christ. The accession is proclaimed in heaven; but the victory is not yet made manifest on earth. 'A king may be a king *de jure*, but he is not a king *de facto* until the trumpet which announces his accession is answered by the acclamation of a loyal and obedient people' (Caird). The tag, *de facto*, originates in acts or deeds. In a sense the coronation is confirmed in the deeds of the Christians, who are to share the reign. But the Christian reigns from a tree. That, for the Christian, is the central fact of history.

In the cross of Christ I glory,
Towering o'er the wrecks of time;
All the light of sacred story
Gathers round its head sublime.

For the cross is the sign of God's judgement and mercy. The elders' hymn spells out the consequence. The time is ripe for judgement and the dissolution of evil. The martyrs need not fear. And, as the Divine Patience weights the scales of justice on the side of mercy, neither need anyone who, belatedly or dimly, recognizes the 'greatness of God in heaven'. In any case the real issue is with 'those who destroy the earth': Babylon and the Beast.

The archetype of the heavenly temple is revealed, showing the Ark of the Covenant. This great treasure, the symbol of God's presence with the Chosen People, had been lost during the Babylonian troubles. In the old Temple it was screened by a curtain, behind which the High Priest was allowed to go once a year. Now here it is again restored (by the obedience of Jesus Christ unto death) to the new Temple, which is the Church. At the moment when the New Covenant was sealed, 'the curtain hanging in the Temple was torn in two, from top to bottom. The earth shook, the rocks split apart' (Matthew 27:51). So here the assumption of power is followed by tremendous consequences.

The Woman and the Dragon 12:1–18

When the thunder-clouds part two mysterious sights (lit. 'great signs') appear in the sky. The first is that of a woman, dazzling with cosmic splendour, and crowned with stars. She is also pregnant. Readers who think that here *at last* is a symbol they can understand – the Virgin Mary – will be disappointed. Unfortunately, she owes more to 2 Esdras, where a sorrowful lady turns into a New Jerusalem (cf. 9:38 – 10:58) than the infancy stories. Eventually she will meet the other Woman, the Mistress of Metropolis, and when she has disposed of her she will become both the Bride of Christ and the New Jerusalem. But for now she has to do with a 'red dragon', also crowned, but with temporal power of some destructiveness, as he has been responsible for the downfall of other temporal powers ('dragged a third of the stars out of the sky'), his seven heads suggesting the seven hills of Rome. Clearly, the source of John's vision is in ancient mythology; probably two stories combine: one, a solar myth, where the sun battles with the dragon of darkness, and the other the well-known motif of the 'stolen prince'. (Such tales correspond with deep-seated social and psychic needs or they would not form such a universal aspect of every culture, from primitive man to Disneyland.) But to what purpose does John use these 'mysterious sights'?

His use of tenses exacerbates the puzzle. We are now in the past again, long before the time of Jesus. The woman with the twelve stars is the Divine Community, in particular the Faithful Remnant of the Chosen People, into which the Messiah was eventually born. The dragon stands over the woman in order to eat her child as soon as it is born. But the child is snatched away and taken to a safe place – 'to God and his throne'; it is the Messiah's faithfulness unto death which, paradoxically, puts him out of death's way. But the Divine Community, the New Israel, is still at risk, and is taken to 'the desert, to a place God has prepared for her'. Now to the Jew the desert was a place of terror, deprivation, and danger. He had not our longing to 'get away from it all' to the wide open spaces. But there had been a time when the desert was a sweet alternative to urban captivity, and that was when the Chosen People were in Egypt. This appears to be the nuance here, reinforced by the fact that scholars calculated 42 stations of the wanderings, corresponding to the 42 months of protection during the persecution. For the Church 'the desert' is anywhere beyond the suburbs of Metropolis; indeed, even the oasis of being 'in', yet not 'of' it.

And now war breaks out in heaven. Dr Caird makes the interesting suggestion that this is the celestial version of what has happened/is happening on earth while Jesus was upon it. 'When the victory is being won in heaven, Christ is on earth on the cross. Because he is part of the earthly reality, he cannot at the same time be part of the heavenly symbolism.' This is ingenious, but as the passage only points up what has been fairly well established before, namely the kingship of Jesus, originating in Psalm 2, it could equally well be 'a doublet', bearing out the Jerusalem Bible scholars' suggestion that *Revelation* may be two apocalypses written by John at different times and put together here. Be that as it may, we get good value for money: a description of the dragon 'that old serpent, named the Devil, or Satan, that deceived the whole world'. Satan began life as a kind of roving public prosecutor whose job was to accuse men before the heavenly court (Job 1:6) where he was once an angel. (In fact the whole of Satanology is an attempt to solve the problem of the origin of evil.) But then he got ideas above his station and became the enemy of God and man. Here he is again, standing before the throne, up to his old tricks, 'the accuser of our brothers'; but – and this is the vital point – there is no use in accusing anybody in heaven, because everybody's status there is 'covered' by the victory of the blood of the Lamb. All who believe in his name are pronounced not guilty, but 'righteous'. This is what the Epistle to the Romans is all about. In some respects it raises the problem of the Divine Comedy of Mistaken Identity. Men did not know what they were doing. They would not have crucified the Lord of Glory. This is the great 'mystery' which *Revelation* is unveiling.

In any event, there is no point in Satan staying on in the heavenly court, because the case is closed. He is thrown out, and, 'filled with rage', comes down to earth. There he will start up practice, embodied as a public prosecutor, when Christians are dragged before tribunals because they will not sacrifice to the imperial goddess, Roma, whom John is anxious to identify as the real dragon, and who will be testy, because the End is not far off and there is 'only a little time left'.

But the Divine Community need have no fear. They must take comfort from that other time when the Chosen People were in a time of trial. Eagles' wings protect 'the woman'; the serpent spurts water (false doctrine) but the earth absorbs it, as it did the reprobates who would not obey Moses (Numbers 16:33). This increases the fury of the dragon who goes off to fight 'against the rest of her descendants'. We leave him on the shore waiting for reinforcements. The Great Attack on the Church is about to be launched.

The Two Beasts 13:1–18

Satan begins by calling up two of his agents. They appear to represent the political and cultic wings of the imperial power, which John is to construe as Antichrist. In Jewish legend there were two monsters. One, who came from the sea, Leviathan, we have already met. The other, who came from the land, was Behemoth. The water-beast went to Asia literally by sea in the shape of the emperor's proconsul. But his badges of office were received at the hands of Daniel (see chapter 7). Here indeed we have an unimaginable creature – the Complete Beast. The notorious Nero rides again: 'the fatal wound' referring to his suicide; its having 'healed', to the rumour that he had not really died but was in exile and would return, or be reincarnated, more terrible than ever. This is confirmed in v. 18 where the figure 666 which, in numerology, means evil personified, is found by the process called *gematria* in the name *Neron Kaesar*.

The whole chapter smacks of recent history: the myth of the still-living Hitler, the need for some hero-leader, the mass hysteria of the Nuremburg rallies – 'the whole earth was amazed and followed after the beast': 'after all, he did give us bread, employment, and the *Autobahn*' – the mark of the star of David, discrimination against non-Aryans, the lies, the blasphemy, the propaganda . . . It is a familiar picture John paints.

However, though the reign of terror is going to be universal, in John's view it is going to be limited in time (the 42 months) and will only take place by God's permission. It is 'allowed'. Everybody will kowtow with the exception of those whose names are written 'in the book of the living that belongs to the Lamb that was killed'. The postscript to the letters is here again, this time more urgently. (Some scholars think the letters were written a good deal earlier than the rest of the apocalypse.) 'Listen, then, if you have ears to hear with!' It is a time which calls for endurance and faith on the part of God's people. They must overcome the evil not by retaliating – surely the meaning of verse 9 – but by taking it upon themselves. This was the way of the Lamb that was killed. Only so can God's redemptive purpose be furthered.

The earth-beast then appears, a dragon in lamb's clothing. He is the Complete Phoney Prophet and Priest (16:13 and 19:20; Deuteronomy 13:1) and he is up to all the tricks of bogus religion: sorcery, magic, 'ventriloquially' talking images, and other well-tried gimmicks of the emperor cultus. Again, the worship will be universal. The only way to escape death, or indeed social ostracism and professional 'cutting', is to be branded on the forehead and hand (where Jews carried small caskets containing snippets of the Law) with the imperial stamp or number, which was 666. Commentators have pointed out that there may be a reference here to Ezekiel 9:4 and that the mark there would, by the time of John, be written with an X, the sign of Christ and of baptism.

The chapter looks, on the face of it, to envisage a deterministic view of destiny, and an attitude to the state which the rest of the New Testament does not confirm. But we do not necessarily have to assume a predestinarian attitude if we remember that the Asian mind did not have the same obsession with consistency as we do. John has no doubt that the salvation of man is rooted in the totally unmerited compassion of God; but he is equally clear that man must respond. His name may be scrubbed out of the Book of Life (3:5).

Certainly both Paul and 1 Peter say something different about secular power, and regard the State as one of 'the orders' for the preservation of life. They should be obeyed, prayed for, encouraged, criticized and, only in the last resort, when they have become demonic, resisted. John, who is painting the picture in stark colours and in certainty of the approach of the End, has no time for subtleties. The day of resistance is now here. For ...

> 'the profound thought behind these tremendous pictures is that man is made to worship some absolute power, and that if he does not worship the true and real Power behind the universe, he will construct a god for himself and give absolute allegiance to that . . . Men will always give their allegiance to some sort of power and in the last analysis it is always a choice between the power that operates through inflicting suffering, the power of the Beast, and the power that operates through accepting suffering, the power of the Lamb.' (Preston and Hanson, p. 97)

The Song of the Redeemed 14:1–13

Again we round a shoulder of the mountain and see the summit. There, standing on Mount Zion is the Noble Army of Martyrs, 144,000 of them, the full muster of those who were sealed in 7:3. John's almost mercurial vision does not tell us whether they are in heaven or on earth. We do know, however, that Psalm 2 is at the back of his mind, for it is from Mount Zion that the expected Messiah would reign over all the nations of the earth. There the people were expecting a warrior; here, at the head of his army, we find the Lamb.

We discover several things about the martyrs:

a) 'They follow the Lamb wherever he goes', doing battle, by their witness, with the powers that operate on earthly, Metropolitan Man.

b) 'They are the men who have kept themselves pure by not having sexual relationships with women'; that is, virgins; or by indulging in idol worship, or by remaining ceremonially pure (Leviticus 15:16) before doing battle.

c) 'They have never been known to lie; they are faultless': they are not only morally pure now, but they always were! If this means what it says it looks as though heaven will be full of George Washington and a few others! The translation is misleading here. The New English Bible has 'No lie was found in their lips'. When faced by martyrdom they held to the truth and spoke it.

d) 'They sang a new song which only they, who had

been redeemed from the earth, could learn' – their distinctive and unique witness on earth is reflected in a special part of the praise in heaven.

And now, as though the witness of the martyrs is not going to be enough, an angel arrives with 'an eternal message of Good News' – *the* Gospel, the reverse side of which is judgement, entreating the people on earth to make real what, in terror, they did when Metropolis was shaken: 'Fear God, and praise his greatness.' On this verse F. D. Maurice comments, 'Take away the fear of God and he whom you worship contracts to your own dimensions. Only if the love of God were contracted would the horror of separation from him be less.' (Quoted in Preston and Hanson)

Shaken to the foundations before, Metropolis has now collapsed. This is the bad news brought by another angel: 'Great Babylon has fallen!' ('The strong wine of her immoral lust', following the RSV, gets over the difficult 'all nations drink of the wine of the wrath of her fornication' of the AV.)

And now comes a direct threat from another angel. In full view of the Lamb and his angels the apostates and recalcitrants will be punished eternally. We must not let the symbols (fire and sulphur) mollify the grim picture John paints of what man can bring upon himself by his own wilful turning from God, a freedom God will not violate, for he operates with man only through the greatest sensitivity, discretion and consent. Those who respond to the gracious invitation will 'rest from their hard work, because the results of their service go with them' – an emphasis on works which the general determinism of John does not always allow for (cf. 2:23).

The Harvest of the Earth 14:14–20

But it is almost too late. The harvest is to begin – a metaphor which would be meaningful to early Christians (Matthew 13:30; Mark 4:29), with the note of crisis elsewhere (Matthew 3:10, Luke 3:9). Under instructions from two angels who come from the Temple, a heavenly being who 'looks like a man' appears with a sharp sickle to start both the corn and grape harvests. Many scholars suggest that the corn harvest denotes the ingathering of the saints whilst the grape harvest, with its bloody imagery (though 'the flood 200 miles long and about five feet deep' is mysterious) is the sinners' doom. Others would eliminate vv. 15–17 as unnecessary and therefore understand the grape harvest as the action following the threat. But Dr Caird has argued, most persuasively, (op. cit. pp. 192–4) that *both* pictures allude to the ingathering of the martyrs; the grape harvest being necessary to qualify the corn, the sign of the coming of the Kingdom, by specifying its mode: martyrdom. Part of his argument originates in the 'first-fruits', which make the whole crop acceptable, and he emphasizes the words 'the winepress outside the city'. Judgement would surely start at the city-centre and we have learned from 12:6 that the martyrs are being prepared 'outside the city' in a spiritual oasis free from metropolitan contamination. It was also there that Jesus, for good and all, achieved the all-effective martyrdom (Hebrews 13:12–13).

> There is a green hill far away,
> Without a city wall . . .

Francis Alexander's devastatingly simple hymn is probably the most precise and peerless exposition of the theology of *Revelation.* For he realizes that the terrible result of divine judgement in history, where everything false will be destroyed, is the other face of The Everlasting Mercy.

The Angels with the Last Plagues 15:1–8

And now the river of blood flowing from the winepress of God's wrath becomes a sea of red: the 'sea of glass, mixed with fire', ruddled by the setting sun. The seven angels with the seven plagues – 'the final expression of God's wrath' – hint at allusions to the Exodus, and what happened at the other Red Sea when, in a critical deliverance, the Dunkirk of the chosen people, the Israelites were saved from both the Beast of Egypt and the Beast of the Deep. And here we find them, 'those who had won the victory', not only across the Red Sea, but the river Jordan, too, landed 'safe on Canaan's side'. They are beyond reach of any of the powers on earth where, we must remember, the Beast has been permitted temporary triumph. To the accompaniment of harps they sing their own version of the Song of Moses (cf. Exodus 15:1ff – one of the oldest bits of the Bible.)

The song expresses confidence that all men will be led to worship the one true God, because they will acknowledge the justice of what he has done. John sees 'the temple in heaven open, with the tent of God's presence in it'. 'Presence', literally means 'witness'. Where the tablets of the Law were (the Law or Torah virtually had personality) there was God. 'Where seven men occupy themselves with Torah', goes one of the sayings of the Jewish Fathers, 'there the Shekinah (a majestic cloud representing God's presence or glory) is with them.' So, amid all the accoutrements of divine glory and power, the seven angels who had mixed incense with the prayers of the faithful before delivering an earlier set of plagues, now take bowls (the word could mean urns) and prepare to pour them over earth. God is sometimes present as his Law. And his law works inexorably. For 'God is not mocked'.

The Bowls of God's Wrath 16:1–21

The executors of God's wrath, coming from the Temple, must therefore be acting under his express orders. Everybody else has been expelled (15:8). The voice coming from the Temple must therefore be his. He himself takes control, as this is to be the last series of plagues, and not to be interrupted. Later the same voice will say: 'It is done.' Metropolis – Babylon, Rome, the Beast or Satan's incarnation – is to be brought down. Again the plagues resemble the plagues of Egypt but some were traditional omens of the Last Days. No commentary is necessary to bring out the reality which lies behind the symbols. They speak for themselves. The starving thousands of Bangladesh and Calcutta, bodies floating down the rivers of Vietnam; Angola, Cyprus, the Middle East, Ulster, Watergate – the pathetic kaleidoscope of our own world is reflected. It all sounds familiar and indicates the collapse of a civilization from one of Toynbee's classical causes: internal weakness and corruption, accompanied by pressure from outside.

The sixth angel hints at what the outside pressures may

be: the Parthian hordes, perhaps with a mad *Nero redivivus* at their head, the fording of the river made easy, like the crossing of Jordan. That trinity of unholiness (the Dragon, the Earth Beast and the Sea Beast) breathe unclean spirits: lies, propaganda, preposterous claims. The Devil has his own Secret Service. The hordes look 'like frogs', an allusion to a distinctively Egyptian plague, and through that to the new oppressor who will not let John's people go. It appears as though, through specious diplomacy, some carefully contrived coalition of forces is being prepared to confront Babylon with a mighty show of arms for the war of the Great Day of God.

So forces muster for Armageddon, the meaning of which nobody seems to know. But wait . . . so terrifying is the agenda of destruction that, during plague five, the altar had to step in to make clear that it was 'true and righteous'; in other words, this is what happens if men will go on ignoring fundamental moral laws. Now there is another voice: that of Jesus himself. In a dramatic intervention he warns his people to be ready, with their clothes at hand, like the Chosen People on Passover Night – for he is coming.

The seventh angel tips out his bowl. The voice of God says, 'It is done'. Judgement Day for Babylon is here. Amidst natural catastrophes of unprecedented ferocity Babylon falls, and with her the cities of all (heathen) countries. The seven plagues end with a bombardment of massive hailstones. Men complain. But they do not repent. So it cannot yet be the End.

The Great Prostitute 17:1–18

Nor is it the End. For the Great Prostitute must be brought to book, and John is invited by an angel to accompany him to the desert to witness her exposure and destruction. In the harsh light of the desert, compared with the shady city brothel, she can be seen for what she is. She arrives on a red beast inscribed with obscene graffiti. Beside the immaculate gown of the Bride of Christ her drag is pretentious (imperial purple), seductive (sinful red), and flashy (gold ornaments). It does not conceal that underneath all the trappings there is a rather faded old whore. Is this what *Roma Aeterna* has come to? for that is who she is. *We* know the identity of the secret name written on her forehead.

However, it looks as though a later editor wanted to make quite sure that the readers could identify the Emperor Domitian as the Antichrist and so, in the following verses, he sharpens the impact by trying to 'predict' history from a fictitious standpoint in 'the past'. There is no need to follow or tease out his elaborate argument. It is a tortured way of proving that the eighth emperor is the phantom Nero: Domitian. He meant well. And he makes a good point in showing that the kings who fornicated with the prostitute will end up by devouring her. So does evil wreak its own destruction. So does God use cynical, secular power to achieve his own ends.

The Fall of Babylon 18:1–19:4

There is a flash of almost atomic splendour and another angel intones a threnody celebrating Babylon's doom. It vibrates with remarkable evocative power. Image after image, graphic, immediate, and compelling are strung together. They give a grim picture of a city in ruins. It is an up-to-date portrait, virtually documentary, of what may happen when you write 'never having had it so good' into the bill of human rights, idolize the gross national product, worship growth, and become so preoccupied with quantity that you ignore quality and, with almost blatant banality, substitute *Benediction* with the Stock Exchange closing prices. It is sufficient to stab the annual service of the Chamber of Commerce into stunned silence. Trade finishes. Business by land and sea collapses. The wheels of industry grind to a halt. The arts fall into decline. Even human relationships disappear from the scene. Hordes of unemployed look on in anxiety and join in the lament at this shambles, this ghost town, this metropolitan *Marie Celeste*. 'Pity cracks the heart.'

But it does not quite crack John's heart. For the dirge indicates that the doom was deserved, for Babylon did not realize on what a sandy foundation her luxuriant living was based. Greedy for power and glory, she thought these made for security. 'Here I sit, a queen! . . . I will never know grief.' John knows that any city which puts faith in the amenities of life and does not understand the contingent character of human existence, and those qualities which transcend the immediate, is doomed. Such a city is a suburb of Chaos, and merits the Deep. And that is where Babylon is despatched (cf. Jeremiah 50–51). So much for the deceitfulness of riches.

But riches were not the immediate cause of Babylon's doom; only the symptom. Babylon was destroyed because she did not recognize the things which belonged to her peace. Otherwise she would have recognized the tokens of that peace in God's people. But she did not, and in a rhapsody celebrating her downfall God's people are commanded paradoxically to 'Come out from her' and to 'pay her back twice as much as she has done' – not even the *lex talionis* (an eye for an eye) will do. We must remember, though, that Babylon symbolized palpable evil, which cannot exist in the presence of God. And it is with that in our minds, with the smoke of the ruins still billowing upwards, that we join the company of praise for the Service of Thanksgiving, and celebrate 'the victory of love over everything that stands in love's way' (Caird).

It soon becomes clear, as the mighty chorus of 'God Be Praised' (lit. Hallelujah, used uniquely here in the New Testament) echoes and re-echoes round heaven, that one chapter is being closed for another to open. When the pall of smoke lifts we shall be given a glimpse of a new order. So we must get ready for the closing acts of the great drama.

The Wedding Feast of the Lamb 19:5–10

Now that the disagreeable wanton and her paramours have been got rid of it is time to prepare for 'the wedding of the Lamb'. The notion of the God/Man relationship as marriage would not surprise John's readers. It was common in pagan practice, well-known in the Old Testament (Hosea 2) and the teaching of Jesus (Matthew 25:1–13, Mark 2:19–20). Moreover Jewish messianic expectation looked forward to a Wedding Feast which would be succeeded by a period of rejoicing and plenty.

To contrast with the brazen costume of the Great Prostitute the bride 'has been given clean shining linen to dress herself with'. It is not necessarily white, but it *is* clean, and clean clothing has come to signify martyrdom and sanctity (3:4; 7:14; 15:6). So the next sentence is no surprise. 'The linen is the righteous deeds of God's people.' The shrouds of the martyrs are thus made into the wedding garment of the Bride of Christ. It has been pieced together by those who have put off 'anger, passion, and hateful feelings' and 'put on . . . humility, gentleness, and patience' (Colossians 3:8,12). But, even so, the dress has been 'given'. The martyr is the first to admit that he is 'clothed upon' with a glory not his own:

> Their beauty this, their glorious dress,
> Jesus, the Lord, our righteousness.

Overcome with this revelation John falls down at the feet of the angelic messenger. He is told to get to his feet again as martyr prophets are co-equal with angels in the sight of God. (There is some evidence of angel-worship, Colossians 2:18.) Truth is one in heaven and on earth. Heavenly message and earthly witness both have their ground in the same Being.

But the consummation is not yet. We await the arrival of the groom.

The Rider on the White Horse 19:11–21

When the bridegroom finally arrives he does so in the uniform of a warrior, riding a white charger, with behind him an army of cavalry – suggestive of scenes from *Alexander Nevsky*, Eisenstein's powerful epic. He is presented as the Victorious One, and the descriptions draw together several other passages. There can be no doubt that he is the Expected One, his 'many crowns' signifying unlimited power and authority. He *is* the Word of God, the Word that assisted at the Creation, summing up all the 'And God saids', the Word testified to in the prophet's words, the Word made flesh, the Word that brought the Church into being and sustains it in the hour of trial. He is the Word which accomplishes what it signifies, a notion difficult to understand in a propaganda-public-relations-ridden world which uses words to cover up the truth. And this

Word is his weapon, for the 'sharp sword' comes out of his mouth. Just as it judges the Church so will it 'defeat the nations'. He is *the Word of God* to the Church; he is *King of Kings and Lord of Lords* to the earth.

Yet there is a significant difference between his uniform and that of his troops: theirs is 'clean white linen'; his is 'covered with blood'. But there has been no fighting. Is this his own blood, by which the critical battle has already been won; or that of his army of martyrs by which they have been incorporated into his messianic mission? Or may it mean both? We do not know for certain. What we do know is that when he does appear, the Messiah comes as Redeemer, Judge, and Lord.

And now a quite hideously revolting scene – suggested by Jewish apocalyptic hope (Ezekiel 39:17ff) – pictures the birds of the air gorging themselves on the carcasses of the earthmen. Their leaders, the beast and the false prophet, are arrested. Though the 'kings of the earth' show their collective political power, there is no real battle. They and their retinue succumb to the Word of Christ. But they are only bit-players ('their armies' is literally 'the rest of them') and are not incinerated, like the principals, in an apparently annihilating 'fire that burns with sulphur'. Their bodies are left for the birds.

The Thousand Years 20:1–6

Though his two chief executives have been disposed of, Satan himself – 'that old serpent' – is still on the loose. The angelic warden of the abyss (cf. 9:1) catches him, binds him, and locks him up for a thousand years.

And so we arrive at the thorny problem of the Millennium over which many battles have raged, for no other part of the New Testament refers to it. Apart from the difficulty of envisaging an earthly reign of such a span, it looks as though evil has yet some part to play (by permission) in the economy of redemption when it appeared to have been scotched for ever.

Difficult though it may be, we must try to see the 1000-year rule against the background of Jewish expectancy, which was composed of two strands; the first, what we call the *eternal weekend*, which took root before the Jews had a firm notion of life after death, saw the period following the Messiah's arrival as one of unmitigated happiness, richness, rest, and the good things of this life; the second, what we may call the *big bang*, held temporal life to be so riddled with sin and, impatient of renewal, looked for a messianic invasion, a limited rule, as a prelude to the abolition of heaven and earth. (Readers who have access to a Bible with the Apocrypha will find such a vision in 2 Esdras 7.) John tries to combine both these views with a vindication of God's sovereignty which gives the martyrs their share of a long earthly rule before the abolition of evil, the winding-up of heaven and earth, and the introduction of a new dimension of being – the New Jerusalem.

The martyrs had been pretty anxious about when they were going to get their reward. During the millennium 'those who had been executed because they had proclaimed the truth' are given a taste of glory. *Glory* carries a meaning other than splendour, as in 'glorious Technicolour'. It can also mean 'being regarded or noted'. When, in 21:24, 'the kings of the earth will bring their wealth' into the New Jerusalem the word used is 'glory'. Wealth then, as now, meant status. So the martyrs have status, and they exercise it in three ways; for they are 'brought back to life' to be judges, kings, and priests; just as their witness was 'incorporated' into the victory of Christ, so now they take their share in a collegiate exercise of rule and redemption amongst the nations which still exist. What this means precisely is not at all clear, but some kind of *dominion* over earthmen is envisaged. Nor is it evident in what form the martyrs would carry out their exalted office. In reconstituted bodies? Dr Caird, at least, thinks not, insisting that as they have already put off the coils of mortality and donned their resurrection robes and just as the resurrected Christ was both seated at his Father's throne yet at the same time omnipresent in his churches, so the martyrs' reign is of the same order, but not the same degree, and 'resurrection means that they have been "let loose into the world".' They may thus be the official residents of the 'colonies of heaven' on earth.

The Defeat of Satan 20:7–10

The thousand years soon pass, with disappointingly little documentation of the era's quality of life, and the time has come to give evil its last fling. Satan is 'set loose from his prison', and starts his nefarious deeds. Soon an enormous global battle has been arranged. The campaign is suggested by Ezekiel (38, 39) who tells of Gog, from the land of Magog, sweeping down on Israel, which had long since recovered from her desolation and was enjoying a period of almost unprecedented prosperity and peace. Is there a hint here that, so pervasive is sin, so subtle and deceptive its ways, even those who are sitting on Zion's hill may still be at risk, by thinking they themselves have achieved security, and thus corrupting the good, when the only ultimate security rests in the gift of God's grace?

That they are at risk seems to be indicated by the description of the nations, 'as many as the grains of sand on the seashore' surrounding the 'camp' – for the people of God are still on pilgrimage – and 'the city that he loves', which comes to the same thing as we shall see, for he 'tents' in both. But Gog and his hordes are incinerated, and the Devil is also despatched to join his henchmen in the everlasting fire. This is the end of the Old Pretender. Everything can now be made new. But who is going to have a place in the New Order? Only the final judgement can reveal that.

The Final Judgement 20:11–15

In Elgar's oratorio, *The Dream of Gerontius*, the soul approaching the Judgement Seat is propelled forward by urgent, disturbing music, which breaks off abruptly. Silence. A shattering chord of cymbals and drums. After a moment's quietness the Soul sings, 'Take me away, take me away, and in the lowest depths there let me lie'. Elgar had some reservations about using the chord, thinking it might be better to leave the listener to fill in the vision – what the Soul saw – from his own imagination. John does exactly this. He says simply, 'I saw a large white throne and the one who sits on it.' In previous chapters he has left plenty of material for the imagination to work on, and therefore makes no attempt to document the appearance of a Being so radiant and consuming that in his presence both heaven and earth vanish like dew before the sun. What he does note is the countless souls who, having undergone 'the first death', are brought to life for the Final Judgement. Death, the sea, Hades, the place of departed spirits, give up their dead. Then death itself, the 'last enemy' which stands between the soul and immortality (1 Corinthians 15:26, 54) is itself destroyed 'in the lake of fire'.

Only two volumes are produced at the court of heaven, for in the summing-up only two things count: what man has done with his freedom, and what the Proper Man has done with his. There are thus the *Book of Merit*, which contains a record of a man's deeds and therefore of his deserts; and there is the *Book of Mercy* – the Lamb's Book of Life – where the one deed of Christ, who died to ransom man and save him from his sins, is put to the credit side of man's account. And it is what is written in the Book of Mercy which determines who is annihilated in the 'lake of fire'.

John does not tell us whether any soul confronted by God in glory finally says 'no', though, in 3:5, he hints that it is possible for a name to be scrawled out of the Lamb's book of life. He *does* insist on the reality of Judgement. Though what is written in the Book of Life may show things in a very different light from what is revealed to earthly scrutiny, he never suggests, like Voltaire, that 'God will forgive; forgiving is his trade.' (*Il me pardonnera; c'est son métier.*) That would be sheer sentimentaility, not charity; for it would empty 'witness' of its meaning, and life of its value.

The New Heaven and the New Earth 21:1–22:5

And so at last we arrive at the best-known part of the apocalypse: the vision of the New Heaven and New Earth, the New Jerusalem, and Paradise, deservedly popular with the common people because it caters for that deep-seated yearning for a happy ending, as though they feel in the marrow of their bones that 'Chaos' is not the answer the universe flings back at them when they question whether it has meaning. But it has also been the inspiration of painters and poets. William Blake, who saw it as 'a representation of what eternally exists, really and unchangeably', called it 'stupendous'. And stupendous it is; but the inhabitant of a crowded tenement in Bombay or Johannesburg might be excused a hollow laugh if we told him that a city was the symbol – 'the translucence of the eternal in and through the temporal' (Coleridge) – of supernal bliss. For him the city is the image of hell. For him industrialized, urbanized Metropolis is something to flee from. Modern man craves for the wide open spaces. He wants to get away from it all

The Pull of the City

Yet this desire for a rural utopia is a relatively recent trend and confined almost exclusively to the Western World. Throughout the Third World, with the possible exception of China, people are making for the towns, just as they did in Europe in the Middle Ages, when a proverb ran 'town air makes a man free' and a preacher could liken the Faith to the city because it offered security, freedom, and unity.

Citizens today, isolated on ribbon roads, often living in crowded loneliness, exposed to vandalism and barbarism, having no significant part in the life of the 'polis' find it incredible that the City was once the image of the Good Life. Yet it is just these people on packaged tours who each year throng the great medieval towns like York, Chester, Dubrovnik, Carcassonne, and Florence, as though some deep-seated emotional and psychological needs were satisfied by the architecture of such places: the rhythm of containment and surprise, the hints of mystery, the winding streets leading to an open place, dominated by a temple pointing to transcendance, a place of interchange and exchange, a whole world of value projected in stone and space. So it looks as though the yearning for an urban paradise is just as insistent as the urge to get back to a lost Eden. In any event John is using a powerful symbol but it is York and Dubrovnik and the other medieval towns we must have in mind, not Detroit, Coventry, or Calcutta. And he includes a garden in his vision for good measure.

The Hope of a New Deal

John, as we shall see, caters for both. What John sees is not the old heaven and earth transformed – they have both 'disappeared' – but a totally new cosmos. We must presume that characteristics are the same, at least to some degree, otherwise the new world would be unrecognizable. But there is one significant difference: there is no sea. The cruel sea, the habitat of all that is evil, that which separates God from his people, has gone for good, setting him free to be really with those who love him. And this is what is about to happen for, as though to underline that this is that 'far off divine event to which the whole creation moves', God himself is to speak, v. 5, and to say that this renovation of the universe is his gift and deed. Moreover he assures John that he must note the divine authority for the hope of a new deal. In spite of everything in the contingent circumstances of his people, notwithstanding persecution, ostracism, and ignominy, God's people must go on trusting him. And they can, for he is the ground of all their being. He is Lord of History. But he, with a universe to govern, will nourish his children, and enter into the most personal relationship with them – that of a father. But those who succumb to emperor worship (to which the catalogue of sins relates) will go into 'the lake burning with fire and sulphur, which is the second death'.

John needed an alternative attractive enough to keep the waverers from succumbing, and he finds it in the picture of the bliss awaiting 'whoever wins the victory' in the New Jerusalem.

The Two Jerusalems

The old earthly Jerusalem had been a place of no consequence. It was set on a modest hill but was not of any strategic value. It was rather inaccessible, and not near trade routes or natural resources. No one thought of developing it until the Ark of the Covenant was moved there. It then became significant as the place of the Presence, a Royal City, and the symbol of Jewish hope. And it retained this place in the heart of the Chosen

People in good times and in bad, even when the Ark had been lost or destroyed. When a Jew thought of the good time coming his hopes centred on Jerusalem. One day it will get into the big time and exercise power among nations (Isaiah 60:11–14); it will look marvellous (Isaiah 54:11–12); it will be the centre of a new order (Isaiah 2:1–4) which the people will obey (Isaiah 60:21); it will be irradiated by the Divine Presence (Isaiah 60:19); the life of the people will be free from anything that may harm them (Isaiah 25:8). Such was Isaiah's prophecy. But Ezekiel added the dream of a New Temple, and gave the most detailed specifications (Ezekiel 40ff) of a new centre for God's saving action (Ezekiel 36:25ff), for he would not allow even Israel's sin to prevent his intention of making the Chosen People a vehicle of grace for all nations (Ezekiel 37:27–28).

By the time John wrote other voices had been added to these through the inter-testamental apocalyptic writings, most – though not all – looking for a realization of the dream on the old earth. A few regarded the creation of this ideal as beyond the possibility of earthmen to achieve and therefore looked for it in heaven. Their view was shared by those who had come under the influence of Plato's philosophy and looked upon all things as mere copies of their corresponding 'ideal realities' which existed in heaven eternally. Everything was thus the anti-type of an ideal. And so the New Jerusalem could be conceived as continuously impinging as an ideal reality through its copy on earth. In fact it sometimes looks as though the notion of an ideal state which stands at the end of time (a catastrophic, final coming, which is Hebrew) and one which is continually being realized (an idealistic, continuous coming, which is Greek) exists in John's thought at one and the same time. If so, perhaps Paul was expressing something of the same kind in the Letter to the Galatians when he says (4:26), 'the heavenly Jerusalem (lit. the Jerusalem *above*) is free, and she is our mother'. (There is a similar allusion in Hebrews 12:22.) There may also be a connection between the 'mother' and the strange city-woman alluded to above (p. 74) for 2 Esdras was available roughly at the time that Paul was writing, and another passage from the same work is worth quoting in full for it shows how near to each other were Jewish and Christian apocalypses:

> Many grievous miseries shall befall them that in the last times dwell in the world, because they have walked in great pride. But understand thou for thyself, and of such as be like thee seek out the glory. For unto you is paradise opened, the tree of life is planted, the time to come is prepared, plenteousness is made ready, a city is builded, and rest is allowed, goodness is perfected, wisdom being perfected aforehand. The root of evil is sealed up from you, weakness is done away from you, and death is hidden; hell and corruption are fled into forgetfulness: sorrows are passed away, and in the end is shewed the treasure of immortality. Therefore ask thou no more questions concerning the multitude of them that perish. For when they had received liberty, they despised the Most High, thought scorn of his law, and forsook his ways. Moreover they have trodden down his righteous, and said in their heart, that there is no God; yea, and that knowing they must die . . . For the Most High willed not that man should come to nought: but they which he created have themselves defiled the name of him that made them. (8:50–60)

A New Heaven and a New Earth

These people, then, felt that they stood at the end of an age. And Christian expectancy was expressed in 2 Peter 3:10–15. 'On that Day the heavens will disappear with a shrill noise, the heavenly bodies will burn up and be destroyed, and the earth with everything in it will vanish . . . God has promised: new heavens and a new earth, where righteousness will be at home.'

We must now examine the way that John takes these contemporary motifs and transposes them into the key of Jesus Christ, remembering all the time that his primary purpose is pastoral, and the vivid pictures which he paints are to nerve Christians against apostasy which, in his view, is literally a fate worse than death.

Once again in a trance he is taken by an angel up to a high mountain (the zenith, of which Babylon, 'sitting on the waters', is the nadir) and told that he is going to be allowed to see 'the Bride, the wife of the Lamb'. But when he looks, as with the Lion and the Lamb, there is something completely different: the New Jerusalem, splendid, dazzling with the blush of consummation, for the city is 'shining with the glory of God'.

In what, then, does the glory consist?

Immediately we are grasped by its physical splendour, and this in two ways:

a) Its materials are of the most dazzling and spectacular order. It scintillates. It dazzles. It shines 'like a precious stone, like a jasper, clear as crystal'. The streets and squares are paved 'of pure gold, as clear as glass'. It is a city whose radiance is so magnificent that it looks to have been carved out of pure light. In the words of current psychology it is 'limbic intensive'.

b) But the splendour is also manifest in its lines and spatial relationships which are perfect. It is so well laid out that, like any properly proportioned city, it resolves all the diverse and contradictory elements in it. It is holistic. Students of *gematria* or 'sacred geometry' find from the information John gives them that it appears to obey the requirements of the ancient laws of aesthetics John Michell, in *City of Revelation*, has constructed dial grams of great beauty, and deduced from some of the- proportional relationships a number which is found in the words *Jesus Christ*. For, just as 666, the number for total imperfection, was found in *Nero*, the perfect number was found in *Jesus Christ*. It appears from recent research that the medieval cathedral tried to be an earthly copy of the heavenly city, and the proportions are found in such magnificent buildings as Chartres. This is now part of architectural common knowledge.

The Meaningful Past

So much for the physical specifications. What about its associations? It is rooted in 'significant soil' for it points to a meaningful past. On the gates are 'written the names of the twelve tribes of the people of Israel', with all that that means both for their rightful successors in the new Israel, and the hint of a hope that even the Jews may be included at the last. There is, moreover, one bit of that significant past symbolized in part of the perfect proportions. For the city is a cube 'as wide and as high as it was long'. The angel had a measuring stick and is measuring the city, so John recalls the measuring that took place when Ezekiel was taken up into a mountain, shown the New Jerusalem, and a man measured not the city, but the Temple. The Holy of Holies in the Temple of Solomon was a perfect cube and made of pure gold (1 Kings 6:20). So the Tabernacle, the place of God's real Presence, is now the City of God. He has really come to his people. There is no longer any need for the curtain that screens the Presence from the People, for 'Now God's home is with men!'

So John has not simply re-pristinized the old hope of New Jerusalem; but he shows God as re-presented to his people. And his presence is a guarantee of bliss. Not only is there a negation of everything that is likely to harm his people – pain, death, grief, crying – for all these have vanished. But there is also a plentiful supply of nourishment from a restored Eden. There is the tree which was the occasion, though not the cause, of so much trouble, now providing abundant fruit. There is perhaps also a hint of that tree which stands in the middle of the Bible, and of which Simone Weil wrote, 'Adam and Eve sought for divinity in vital energy – a tree, fruit. But it is prepared for us on dead wood, geometrically squared, where a corpse is hanging . . . I have to be like God, but like God crucified.'

Gods is All in All

There is an equally never-ending supply of water from the river of the Water of Life which, since it comes from the throne of God and the Lamb, is the life of God himself. There is no need to fear the serpent. It has gone with everything else on which 'God's curse' was placed.

There is, naturally, no Temple, for it was the function of the Temple to demarcate the holy – that which was possessed by God – from that which was not. Now his presence is ubiquitous. He is in everything. He is all in all. Dante must have felt like John when, at the conclusion of his vision, he

saw how love held bound
Into one volume all the leaves whose flight
Is scattered through the universe around.
For everything the will has ever sought
Is gathered there, and there is every quest
Made perfect, which apart from love falls short.
Paradiso, Canto XXXIII (Penguin)

Thus, in the New Jerusalem, everything exists 'in' God. Now the old distinction between the sacred and the secular has been done away. The New Jerusalem is the completion of that 'at homeness' of God with his people which began when Jesus 'yielded up his spirit . . . and behold, the veil of the temple was rent in twain from the top to the bottom' (Matthew 27:50, 51). At that moment religion was secularized; everything became potentially the vessel of holiness. Just as the Great Harlot's presence in Babylon polluted everything, even those things which were 'good', so the Presence in the New Jerusalem fulfils Zechariah's prophecy (14:21) and every pot is holy.

No Temple and No Religion

As there is no Temple, for the City is the Temple, it is difficult to know where the Throne is. John does not say. But he is clear that, among other things, the New Order will afford something that was never possible under the Old Order. For then God's face was regarded as too holy for men to gaze upon (Exodus 33:20). Now they will see him face to face. They will be afforded the *summum bonum*. They will see him whom no man has seen at any time, but who has been 'declared' in the Son. Those who recognized him in the *incognito* of the crucified Jesus will 'know him and enjoy him for ever'. 'For his name is written on their foreheads,' And to receive the name is to share in the life. 'Naming' does not impart a label, but a nature.

The experience of the early Church was that 'when two or three were gathered together' in the name of Jesus, they were made vividly aware of his continued presence with them, sometimes in a way which was almost tangible, and so convinced were they that it was the Presence in its fullness that they could affirm 'Jesus is Lord.' And it was on that creed that the early Church took its stand. So we are not surprised to find that the foundation stones of the walls of the city are the twelve apostles, for it was the apostolic faith (the 'deposit' which Paul urged Timothy to guard) which was the token of catholicity and a bulwark against heresy. And in order to ram home this truth, John takes the precious jewels which had been associated with the old order (as embellishments to the High Priest's breastplate) and gives them to the apostles. (Just to rid them of the astrological associations which they carried, he distributes them in the reverse of the astrological order.) Zechariah had predicted that the city would be protected, not by tangible walls, but by the burning presence of God. And so indeed it is, but not in the way he would have expected. The honour of the bride, and the safety of the city, are kept by the burning zeal of the apostolic church.

The Old Sanctified in the New

The apostolic walls, looking upon the New Jerusalem and towards the 'outside', make a sort of interim symbol between that which was – the old order, that which is – the new order; and that which is to be, for they are pierced by twelve gates, undoubtedly reminiscent of the twelve tribes. 'The gates of the city will stand open all day.' They never close. The walls keep out every person and every thing which does not qualify for residence, and John is prepared to admit nothing which will lower the quality of life; but he clearly hopes that even the most unpromising and intractable earthmen may in the end find their way through the gates. He even sees the possibility that 'the kings of the earth', who had lain with the whore of Babylon, may one day bring 'the wealth of the nations' into it. 'Nothing from the old order which is of value in the sight of God is debarred from entry into the new' (Caird). Indeed, even within Paradise, there is medicine for the sick of soul, for 'the leaves (of the tree of life) are for the healing of the nations'. Outside the wall lies the mission field. The apostles, and those who follow in their steps, draw their strength from within the city, but they are sent out.

The Bride and the Local Church

For all this heady language, the glittering panorama of eternal bliss, must not distract our attention from the fact that what John is describing is a metaphor for the Bride of Christ, the Divine Community; and the New Jerusalem has its suburbs in Smyrna and wherever the Church is, even 'the half-finished, sham Gothic erection on the new housing estate' as C. S. Lewis's Screwtape – an apostle of our father below – described the local tabernacle of the Presence.[1] For the citizens of the New Jerusalem live on the outside and the inside at one and the same time, and between the time of the city that already is and the time of the city that is to be. For, as St Augustine put it;

> 'The City of God goes its way as a stranger on earth; it summons citizens from all peoples, and gathers an alien society of all languages. It cares nothing for the differences in the laws and institutions by which earthly peace is gained or maintained. But indeed the heavenly city makes use of the earthly peace. It guards and seeks the merging of human wills and makes earthly peace minister to the heavenly peace . . . And when we arrive thither, there shall be no mortal life, but a life indeed; no animal body to burden the soul with its corruption, but a spiritual body that wants nothing and is wholly subdued to the will. During its earthly pilgrimage the heavenly city enjoys this peace by faith, and it lives justly by this faith by making the life of that city the goal of every good action performed in the service of God and one's neighbour.'

On this view the City of the Presence, the New Jerusalem, exists among, and hobnobs with, the City of Earth, virtually unrecognized, by the quality of its life, which is eternal, impinging on the temporal and, paradoxically, building up the eternal future city which already is. 'Let us even now place ourselves in that victory which is still to come' (Augustine).

The Way to the City

It goes without saying that John does not think it necessary to include in the prospectus of the New

1. *The Screwtape Letters*, C. S. Lewis, Fount

Jerusalem that there are no easy access roads. The easy roads by-pass the city. But there is a pilgrims' way, the *via crucis*. Only the pilgrim who has passed that way has 'the right to eat the fruit from the tree of life, and to go through the gates into the city'.

The Coming of Jesus 22:6–21

And now the voice of Jesus is again heard. He announces that he is himself coming. He whose coming unveiled the grace of God on which the life of the Church is grounded, and unmasked the pretensions of man on which Babylon is precariously founded, repeats that he is coming soon. The Bride and the Spirit bid him to come. The response has clear liturgical and eucharistic overtones. The Eucharist was itself an anticipation of the End; for in the Eucharist past, present and future are made one: he who was is 'brought back', is brought to remembrance, and looks forward to the End. 'I shall not taste of the fruit of the vine until I drink it new with you in my Father's kingdom.' So present time is also End time. And he who was there in the beginning and came, and will come, comes to be the lamp-standard in the midst of his people. He comes in a multitude of ways. He is made present to the believer in the Eucharist, but he also comes as Teilhard de Chardin saw, in that uniting principle in the heart of matter which is painfully bringing the whole universe to that End which God has designed for it; he comes in the political crises of our day when men like Camus recognize him in the bloodstained faces of their generation; he comes sometimes, as he did for Schweitzer, 'as one unknown, without a name'. As he came in lowliness he comes also as Lord of All, Living – And Crucified.

Therefore, Watch!

THE REVELATION TO JOHN

1 In this book are written the things that Jesus Christ revealed. These things were given him by God, for him to show God's servants what must happen very soon. Christ made these things known to his servant John by sending his angel to him. 2 John has told all that he has seen. This is his report concerning the message from God and the truth revealed by Jesus Christ. 3 Happy is the one who reads this book, and happy are those who listen to the words of this prophetic message and obey what is written in this book! For the time is near when all this will happen.

Greetings to the Seven Churches

4 From John to the seven churches in the province of Asia:

Grace and peace be yours from God, who is, who was, and who is to come, and from the seven spirits in front of his throne, 5 and from Jesus Christ, the faithful witness, the first-born Son who was raised from death, who is also the ruler of the kings of the earth.

He loves us, and by his death he has freed us from our sins 6 and made us a kingdom of priests to serve his God and Father. To Jesus Christ be the glory and power for ever and ever! Amen.

7 Look, he is coming with the clouds! Everyone will see him, including those who pierced him. All peoples of earth will mourn because of him. Certainly so! Amen.

8 "I am the Alpha and the Omega," says the Lord God Almighty, who is, who was, and who is to come.

A Vision of Christ

9 I am John, your brother, and in union with Jesus I share with you in suffering, and in his Kingdom, and in enduring. I was put on the island named Patmos because I had proclaimed God's word and the truth that Jesus revealed. 10 On the Lord's day the Spirit took control of me, and I heard a loud voice, that sounded like a trumpet, speaking behind me. 11 It said: "Write down what you see, and send the book to these seven churches: in

Ephesus, Smyrna, Pergamum, Thyatira, Sardis, Philadel-
phia, and Laodicea."
12 I turned round to see who was talking to me. There
I saw seven gold lamp-stands. 13 Among them stood a
being who looked like a man, wearing a robe that reached
to his feet, and a gold band round his chest. 14 His hair
was white as wool, or as snow, and his eyes blazed like
fire; 15 his feet shone like brass melted in the furnace and
then polished, and his voice sounded like a mighty water-
fall. 16 He held seven stars in his right hand, and a sharp
two-edged sword came out of his mouth. His face was as
bright as the midday sun. 17 When I saw him I fell down
at his feet like a dead man. He placed his right hand on
me and said: "Don't be afraid! I am the first and the
last. 18 I am the living one! I was dead, but look, I am
alive for ever and ever. I have authority over death and
the world of the dead. 19 Write, then, the things you see,
both the things that are now, and the things that will
happen afterwards. 20 Here is the secret meaning of the
seven stars that you see in my right hand, and of the seven
gold lamp-stands: the seven stars are the angels of the
seven churches, and the seven lamp-stands are the seven
churches."

The Message to Ephesus

2 "To the angel of the church in Ephesus write:
"This is the message from the one who holds the
seven stars in his right hand, who walks among the seven
gold lamp-stands. 2 I know what you have done; I know
how hard you have worked and how patient you have
been. I know that you cannot tolerate evil men, and that
you have tested those who say they are apostles but are
not, and have found out that they are liars. 3 You are
patient, you have suffered troubles for my sake, and you
have not given up. 4 But here is what I have against you:
you do not love me now as you did at first. 5 Remember
how far you have fallen! Turn from your sins and do what
you did at first. If you don't turn from your sins, I will
come to you and take your lamp-stand from its place.
6 But here is what you have in your favour: you hate what
the Nicolaitans do, as much as I.
7 "If you have ears, then, listen to what the Spirit says
to the churches!

"To those who have won the victory I will give the right to eat the fruit of the tree of life that grows in the Garden of God."

The Message to Smyrna

8 "To the angel of the church in Smyrna write:
"This is the message from the one who is the first and the
last, who died and lived again. 9 I know your troubles; I
know that you are poor — but really you are rich! I know
the evil things said against you by those who claim to be
Jews, but are not; they are a group that belongs to Satan!
10 Do not be afraid of anything you are about to suffer.
Listen! The Devil will put you to the test by having some of
you thrown into prison; your troubles will last ten days. Be
faithful until death, and I will give you the crown of life.

11 "If you have ears, then, listen to what the Spirit says to the churches!
"Those who win the victory will not be hurt by the second death."

The Message to Pergamum

12 "To the angel of the church in Pergamum write:
"This is the message from the one who has the sharp
two-edged sword. 13 I know where you live, there where
Satan has his throne. You are true to me, and you did not
abandon your faith in me even during the time when
Antipas, a faithful witness for me, was killed there where
Satan lives. 14 But here are a few things I have against

you: there with you are some who follow the teaching of Balaam, who taught Balak how to cause the people of Israel to sin by eating food that had been offered to idols, and by committing immorality. [15] In the same way, you also have people among you who follow the teaching of the Nicolaitans. [16] Turn from your sins, then! If not, I will come to you soon and fight against those people with the sword that comes out of my mouth.

[17] "If you have ears, then, listen to what the Spirit says to the churches!

"To those who have won the victory I will give some of the hidden manna. I will also give each of them a white stone, on which a new name is written, which no one knows except the one who receives it."

The Message to Thyatira

[18] "To the angel of the church in Thyatira write:

"This is the message from the Son of God, whose eyes blaze like fire, whose feet shine like polished brass. [19] I know what you do. I know your love, your faithfulness, your service, and your patience. I know that you are doing more now than you did at first. [20] But here is what I have against you: you tolerate that woman Jezebel, who calls herself a messenger of God. She teaches and misleads my servants into committing immorality and eating food that has been offered to idols. [21] I have given her time to turn from her sins, but she does not wish to turn from her immorality. [22] Therefore I will throw her on a bed where she and those who committed adultery with her will suffer terribly. I will do this now, unless they repent from the wicked things they did with her. [23] I will also kill her children, and then all the churches will know that I am he who knows men's thoughts and wishes. I will repay each one of you according to what you have done.

[24] "But the rest of you in Thyatira have not followed this evil teaching; you have not learned what the others call 'the deep secrets of Satan.' I say to you that I will not put any other burden on you. [25] But you must hold firmly to what you have until I come. [26–28] To those who win the victory, who continue to do what I want until the very end, I will give the same authority which I received from my Father: I will give them authority over the nations, to rule

them with an iron rod and to break them to pieces like clay
pots. I will also give them the morning star.
29 "If you have ears, then, listen to what the Spirit says
to the churches!"

The Message to Sardis

3 "To the angel of the church in Sardis write:
"This is the message from the one who has the seven
spirits of God and the seven stars. I know what you are
doing; I know that you have the reputation of being alive,
even though you are dead! 2 So wake up, and strengthen
what you still have, before it dies completely. For I find
that what you have done is not yet perfect in the sight of
my God. 3 Remember, then, what you were taught and
how you heard it; obey it, and turn from your sins. If you
do not wake up, I will come upon you like a thief, and you
will not even know the hour when I come. 4 But a few
of you there in Sardis have kept your clothes clean. You
will walk with me, clothed in white, for you are worthy
to do so. 5 Those who win the victory will be clothed like
this in white, and I will not remove their names from the
book of the living. In the presence of my Father and of
his angels I will declare openly that they belong to me.
6 "If you have ears, then, listen to what the Spirit says
to the churches!"

The Message to Philadelphia

7 "To the angel of the church in Philadelphia write:
"This is the message from the one who is holy and true,
who holds the key that belonged to David, who opens so
that none can close, who closes so that none can open. 8 I
know what you do; I know that you have a little power;
you have followed my teaching and have been faithful to
me. I have opened a door before you, which no one can
close. 9 Listen! As for that group that belongs to Satan,
those liars who claim that they are Jews, but are not, I
will make them come before you and fall down and worship you. They will all know that I love you. 10 Because
you have kept my order to be patient, I will also keep
you safe from the time of trouble which is coming upon
the whole world, to test all the people on earth. 11 I am
coming soon. Keep safe what you have, so that no one will
rob you of your victory prize. 12 I will make him who is

victorious a pillar in the temple of my God, and he will
never again leave it. I will write on him the name of my
God, and the name of the city of my God, the new Jeru-
salem, which will come down out of heaven from my God.
I will also write on him my new name.
13 "If you have ears, then, listen to what the Spirit says
to the churches!"

The Message to Laodicea

14 "To the angel of the church in Laodicea write:
"This is the message from the Amen, the faithful and
true witness, who is the origin of all that God has created.
15 I know what you have done; I know that you are
neither cold nor hot. How I wish you were either one or
the other! 16 But because you are barely warm, neither hot
nor cold, I am about to spit you out of my mouth! 17 'I
am rich and well off,' you say, 'I have all I need.' But you
do not know how miserable and pitiful you are! You are
poor, naked, and blind. 18 I advise you, then, to buy gold
from me, pure gold, in order to be rich. Buy also white
clothing to dress yourself and cover up your shameful
nakedness. Buy also some medicine to put on your eyes,
so that you may see. 19 I reprove and punish all whom I
love. Be in earnest, then, and turn from your sins. 20 Listen!

I stand at the door and knock; if anyone hears my voice
and opens the door, I will come into his house and eat with
him, and he will eat with me. 21 To those who win the
victory I will give the right to sit by me on my throne, just

as I have been victorious, and now sit by my Father on his
throne.
22 "If you have ears, then, listen to what the Spirit says to
the churches!"

Worship in Heaven

4 At this point I had another vision, and saw an open
door in heaven.
And the voice that sounded like a trumpet, which I had
heard speaking to me before, said, "Come up here, and I
will show you what must happen after this." 2 At once
the Spirit took control of me. There in heaven was a
throne, with someone sitting on it. 3 His face gleamed
like such precious stones as jasper and carnelian; all round
the throne there was a rainbow the colour of an emerald.
4 In a circle round the throne were twenty-four other
thrones, on which were seated twenty-four elders dressed
in white, and wearing gold crowns. 5 From the throne
came flashes of lightning, and sounds, and peals of thunder.
There were seven lighted torches burning before the throne;
these are the seven spirits of God. 6 In front of the throne
there was what looked like a sea of glass, clear as crystal.
Surrounding the throne, on each of its sides, were four
living creatures covered with eyes in front and in back.
7 The first living creature looked like a lion; the second
looked like a calf; the third had a face like a man's face;
and the fourth looked like a flying eagle. 8 Each one of
the four living creatures had six wings, and they were
covered over with eyes, inside and out. They never stop
their singing day or night:

"Holy, holy, holy, is the Lord God Almighty,
Who was, who is, and who is to come."

9 As often as the four living creatures sing songs of glory
and honour and thanks to the one who sits on the throne,
who lives for ever and ever, 10 the twenty-four elders fall
down before the one who sits on the throne, and worship
him who lives for ever and ever. They throw their crowns
before the throne, and say:

11 "Our Lord and God! You are worthy
To receive glory, and honour, and power.
For you created all things,
And by your will they were given existence
and life."

The Scroll and the Lamb

5 I saw a scroll in the right hand of the one who sat
on the throne; it was covered with writing on both
sides, and was sealed with seven seals. 2 And I saw a
mighty angel who proclaimed in a loud voice: "Who is
worthy to break the seals and open the scroll?" 3 But no
one was found in heaven, or on earth, or in the world below,
who could open the scroll and look inside it. 4 I cried bit-
terly because no one had been found who was worthy to
open the scroll or to look inside it. 5 Then one of the elders
said to me: "Don't cry. Look! The Lion from Judah's
tribe, the great descendant of David, has won the victory
and can break the seven seals and open the scroll."

6 Then I saw a Lamb standing in the centre of the
throne, surrounded by the four living creatures and the
elders. The Lamb appeared to have been killed. It had
seven horns and seven eyes, which are the seven spirits of
God which have been sent into all the world. 7 The Lamb
went and took the scroll from the right hand of the one
who sat on the throne. 8 As he did so, the four living
creatures and the twenty-four elders fell down before the
Lamb. Each had a harp, and gold bowls filled with in-
cense, which are the prayers of God's people. 9 They sang
a new song:

"You are worthy to take the scroll
And to break open its seals.
For you were killed, and by your death
You bought men for God,
From every tribe, and language, and people,
and nation.
10 You have made them a kingdom of priests to
serve our God;
And they shall rule on earth."

11 Again I looked, and I heard angels, thousands and
tens of thousands of them! They stood round the throne,
the four living creatures, and the elders, 12 and sang in a
loud voice:

"The Lamb who was killed is worthy
To receive power, wealth, wisdom, and
strength,
Honour, glory, and praise!"

13 And I heard every creature in heaven, on earth, and in

the world below, and every creature in the sea — all creatures in the whole universe — and they were singing:

"To him who sits on the throne, and to the
Lamb,
Be praise and honour, glory and might,
For ever and ever!"

14 The four living creatures answered, "Amen!" And the
elders fell down and worshipped.

The Seals

6 Then I saw the Lamb break open the first of the seven
seals, and I heard one of the four living creatures say
in a voice that sounded like thunder: "Come!"
2 I looked,
and there was a white horse. Its rider held a bow, and he
was given a crown. He went out as a conqueror to
conquer.

3 Then the Lamb broke open the second seal; and I
heard the second living creature say: "Come!"
4 Another
horse came out, a red one. Its rider was given the power
to bring war on the earth, that men should kill each other;
he was given a large sword.

5 Then the Lamb broke open the third seal; and I heard
the third living creature say: "Come!" I looked, and
there was a black horse. Its rider held a pair of scales in
his hand.
6 I heard what sounded like a voice coming
from among the four living creatures. It said: "A quart
of wheat for a whole day's wages, and three quarts of
barley for a whole day's wages. But do not damage the
olive oil and the wine!"

7 Then the Lamb broke open the fourth seal; and I
heard the fourth living creature say: "Come!" 8 I looked,
and there was a pale-coloured horse. Its rider was named
Death, and Hades followed close behind. They were given
authority over a fourth of the earth, to kill with sword,
with famine, with disease, and with the wild animals of
earth.

9 Then the Lamb broke open the fifth seal. I saw
underneath the altar the souls of those who had been
killed because they had proclaimed God's word and had
been faithful in their witnessing. 10 They shouted in a
loud voice: "Almighty Lord, holy and true! How long
will it be until you will judge the people of earth and
punish them for killing us?" 11 Each of them was given
a white robe; and they were told to rest a little while
longer, until the total number was reached of their fellow
servants and brothers who were to be killed as they had
been.

12 And I saw the Lamb break open the sixth seal.
There was a violent earthquake, and the sun became
black, like coarse black cloth, and the moon turned com-
pletely red, like blood; 13 the stars fell out of the sky to
earth, like unripe figs falling from the tree when a strong
wind shakes it. 14 The sky disappeared, like a scroll being
rolled up, and every mountain and island was moved from
its place. 15 Then the kings of the earth, the rulers and
the military chiefs, the rich and the mighty, and all other
men, slave and free, hid themselves in caves and under
rocks on the mountains. 16 They called out to the moun-
tains and to the rocks: "Fall down on us and hide us
from the eyes of the one who sits on the throne, and from
the wrath of the Lamb! 17 For the great day of their wrath is
here, and who can stand up against it?"

The 144,000 People of Israel

7 After this I saw four angels standing at the four
corners of the earth, holding back the four winds of
the earth, so that no wind should blow on the earth, or on
the sea, or on any tree. 2 And I saw another angel coming
up from the east with the seal of the living God. He called
out in a loud voice to the four angels to whom God had
given the power to damage the earth and the sea. 3 The

angel said: "Do not harm the earth, or the sea, or the
trees, until we mark the servants of our God with a seal on
their foreheads." [4] And I was told the number of those who
were marked with God's seal on their foreheads: it was
a hundred and forty-four thousand, from every tribe of the
people of Israel. [5] There were twelve thousand from the
tribe of Judah marked with the seal; twelve thousand from
the tribe of Reuben; twelve thousand from the tribe of
Gad; [6] twelve thousand from the tribe of Asher; twelve
thousand from the tribe of Naphtali; twelve thousand from
the tribe of Manasseh; [7] twelve thousand from the tribe of
Simeon; twelve thousand from the tribe of Levi; twelve
thousand from the tribe of Issachar; [8] twelve thousand from
the tribe of Zebulun; twelve thousand from the tribe of
Joseph; and twelve thousand from the tribe of Benjamin.

The Great Crowd

[9] After this I looked, and there was a great crowd—
no one could count all the people! They were from every
nation, tribe, people, and language, and they stood in front
of the throne and of the Lamb, dressed in white robes, and
holding palm branches in their hands. [10] They called out
in a loud voice: "Our salvation comes from our God, who
sits on the throne, and from the Lamb!" [11] All the angels
stood round the throne, the elders, and the four living
creatures. Then they fell down on their faces before the
throne and worshipped God, [12] saying: "Amen! Praise, and
glory, and wisdom, and thanks, and honour, and power,
and might, belong to our God for ever and ever! Amen!"
[13] One of the elders asked me, "Who are those people
dressed in white robes, and where do they come from?"
[14] "I don't know, sir. You do," I answered. He said to me:
"These are the people who have come safely through the
great persecution. They washed their robes and made
them white with the blood of the Lamb. [15] That is why
they stand before God's throne and serve him day and
night in his temple. He who sits on the throne will protect
them with his presence. [16] Never again will they hunger
or thirst; neither sun nor any scorching heat will burn
them; [17] for the Lamb, who is in the centre of the throne,
will be their shepherd, and guide them to springs of living
water; and God will wipe away every tear from their eyes."

The Seventh Seal

8 When the Lamb broke open the seventh seal, there
was silence in heaven for about half an hour. 2 Then
I saw the seven angels who stand before God; they were
given seven trumpets.
3 Another angel, who had a gold incense container, came
and stood at the altar. He was given much incense to add
to the prayers of all God's people and offer on the altar
that stands before the throne. 4 The smoke of the burning
incense went up with the prayers of God's people from the
hands of the angel standing before God. 5 Then the angel
took the incense container, filled it with fire from the altar,
and threw it on the earth. There were peals of thunder,
sounds, flashes of lightning, and an earthquake.

The Trumpets

6 Then the seven angels with the seven trumpets pre-
pared to blow them.
7 The first angel blew his trumpet. Hail and fire, mixed
with blood, came pouring down on the earth. A third
of the earth was burned up, and a third of the trees were
burned up, and every blade of green grass was burned up.
8 Then the second angel blew his trumpet. Something
that looked like a large mountain burning with fire was
thrown into the sea. A third of the sea was turned into
blood, 9 and a third of all living creatures in the sea died,
and a third of all ships were destroyed.
10 Then the third angel blew his trumpet. A large star,
burning like a torch, dropped from the sky and fell on a
third of the rivers, and on the springs of water. 11 (The
name of the star is Bitterness.) A third of the water turned
bitter, and many men died from drinking the water, be-
cause it had turned bitter.
12 Then the fourth angel blew his trumpet. A third of

the sun was struck, and a third of the moon, and a third of the stars, so that their light lost a third of its brightness; there was no light during a third of the day and during a third of the night also.

13 Then I looked, and I heard an eagle that was flying high in the air say in a loud voice: "Oh horror! horror!

How horrible it will be for all who live on earth when the sound comes from the trumpets that the other three angels must blow!"

9 Then the fifth angel blew his trumpet. I saw a star
which had fallen from the sky to earth; it was given
the key to the abyss. 2 The star opened the abyss, and
smoke poured out of it, like the smoke from a large
furnace; the sunlight and the air were made dark by the
smoke from the abyss. 3 Locusts came down out of the
smoke onto the earth, and they were given power like that
of scorpions. 4 They were told not to harm the grass, or the
trees, or any other plant; they could harm only the men
who do not have the mark of God's seal on their foreheads.
5 The locusts were not allowed to kill these men, but only
to torture them for five months. The pain caused by their
torture is like the pain a man suffers when stung by a
scorpion. 6 During the five months those men will seek
death, but will not find it; they will want to die, but death
will flee from them.
7 The locusts looked like horses ready for battle; on their
heads they had what seemed to be gold crowns, and their
faces were like men's faces. 8 Their hair was like women's
hair, their teeth were like lions' teeth. 9 Their chests were
covered with what looked like iron breastplates, and the

sound made by their wings was like the noise of many
horse-drawn chariots rushing into battle. 10 They have
tails and stings, like those of a scorpion, and it is with their
tails that they have the power to hurt men for five months.
11 They have a king ruling over them, who is the angel
in charge of the abyss. His name in Hebrew is Abaddon;
in Greek the name is Apollyon (meaning "The De-
stroyer").

12 The first horror is over; after this there are still two
more horrors to come.

13 Then the sixth angel blew his trumpet. I heard a
voice coming from the corners of the gold altar standing
before God. 14 The voice said to the sixth angel who had
the trumpet: "Release the four angels who are bound at
the great river Euphrates!" 15 The four angels were re-
leased; they had been prepared for this very hour of this
very day of this very month and year, to kill a third of
all mankind. 16 I was told the number of mounted troops:
it was two hundred million. 17 And in my vision I saw the
horses and their riders: they had breastplates red as fire,
blue as sapphire, and yellow as sulphur. The horses' heads
were like lions' heads, and from their mouths came out
fire, smoke, and sulphur. 18 A third of mankind was
killed by those three plagues: the fire, the smoke, and the
sulphur coming out of the horses' mouths. 19 For the
power of the horses is in their mouths, and also in their
tails. Their tails are like snakes, with heads, and they use
them to hurt people.

20 The rest of mankind, all those who had not been
killed by these plagues, did not turn away from what they
themselves had made. They did not stop worshipping the
demons and the idols of gold, silver, bronze, stone, and
wood, which cannot see, or hear, or walk. 21 Nor did
those men repent of their murders, their magic, their im-
morality, or their stealing.

The Angel and the Little Scroll

10 Then I saw another mighty angel coming down out
of heaven. He was dressed in a cloud, with a rain-
bow round his head; his face was like the sun, and his
legs were like columns of fire. 2 He had a small scroll open
in his hand. He put his right foot on the sea, and his
left foot on the land, 3 and called out in a loud voice that

sounded like the roar of lions. After he had called out,
the seven thunders answered back with a roar. 4 As soon
as they spoke, I was about to write. But I heard a voice
speak from heaven: "Keep secret what the seven thunders
said; do not write it down!"
5 Then the angel that I saw standing on the sea and on
the land raised his right hand to heaven 6 and made a
vow in the name of God, who lives for ever and ever, who
created heaven and all things in it, the earth and all things
in it, and the sea and all things in it. The angel said:
"There will be no more delay! 7 But when the seventh
angel blows his trumpet, then God will accomplish
his secret plan, as he announced it to his servants, the
prophets."
8 Then the voice that I had heard speaking from heaven
spoke to me again, saying: "Go and take the open scroll
which is in the hand of the angel standing on the sea and
on the land." 9 I went to the angel and asked him to give
me the little scroll. He said to me, "Take it and eat it; it
will turn sour in your stomach, but in your mouth it will
be sweet as honey." 10 I took the little scroll from his hand
and ate it, and it tasted sweet as honey in my mouth. But
after I had swallowed it, it turned sour in my stomach.
11 Then I was told, "Once again you must speak God's
message about many peoples and nations, languages and
kings."

The Two Witnesses

11 I was then given a measuring stick, like a rod, and
told: "Get up and measure the temple of God and
the altar, and count those who are worshipping in the

temple. 2 But omit the outer courts of the temple. Do
not measure them, for they have been given to the heathen,
who will trample on the Holy City for forty-two months.
3 I will send my two witnesses, dressed in sackcloth; and
they will proclaim God's message during those twelve
hundred and sixty days."

4 The two witnesses are the two olive trees and the two
lamps that stand before the Lord of the earth. 5 If anyone
tries to harm them, fire comes out of their mouths and
destroys their enemies; and in this way whoever shall try
to harm them will be killed. 6 They have authority to
shut up the sky so there will be no rain during the time
they speak God's message. They have authority also over
the springs of water, to turn them into blood; they have
authority also to strike the earth with every kind of plague
as often as they wish.

7 When they finish proclaiming their message, the beast
that comes up out of the abyss will fight against them. He
will defeat them and kill them, 8 and their bodies will lie
on the street of the great city, where their Lord was
nailed to the cross. The symbolic name of that city is
Sodom, or Egypt. 9 People of all nationalities, from every
tribe, language, and nation, will look at their bodies for
three and a half days, and will not allow them to be buried.
10 The people of earth will be happy over the death of
these two. They will celebrate, and send presents to one
another, because those two prophets brought much suffer-
ing upon the people of earth. 11 After three and a half
days a life-giving breath came from God and entered
them, and they stood up; all who saw them were terribly
afraid. 12 Then the two prophets heard a loud voice say
to them from heaven: "Come up here!" As their enemies
watched, they went up into heaven in a cloud. 13 At that
very moment there was a violent earthquake; a tenth of
the city was destroyed, and a total of seven thousand
people were killed in the earthquake. The rest of the
people were terrified and praised the greatness of the God
of heaven.

14 The second horror is over; but look! The third horror
will come soon.

The Seventh Trumpet

15 Then the seventh angel blew his trumpet, and there

were loud voices in heaven, saying, "The power to rule
over the world belongs now to our Lord and his Messiah,
and he will rule for ever and ever!" 16 Then the twenty-
four elders who sit on their thrones before God fell down
on their faces and worshipped God, 17 saying:

"Lord God Almighty, the one who is and who
was!
We thank you that you have used your
great power
And have begun to rule!
18 The heathen were filled with rage,
For it is the time for your wrath to come,
And for the dead to be judged;
The time to give the reward to your servants
the prophets,
And to all your people, great and small,
To all who fear you.
It is the time to destroy those who destroy the
earth!"

19 God's temple in heaven was opened, and the ark hold-
ing the covenant was seen in his temple. Then there were
flashes of lightning, sounds, peals of thunder, an earth-
quake, and heavy hail.

The Woman and the Dragon

12 Then a great sign appeared in heaven: there was a
woman, whose dress was the sun and who had the
moon under her feet, and a crown of twelve stars on her
head. 2 She was soon to give birth, and the pains and
suffering of childbirth made her cry out.

3 Another sign appeared in heaven. There was a huge
red dragon with seven heads and ten horns, and a crown
on each of his heads. 4 With his tail he dragged a third of
the stars out of the sky and threw them to earth. He stood
in front of the woman who was about to give birth, in
order to eat her child as soon as it was born. 5 Then the
woman gave birth to a son, who will rule over all nations
with an iron rod. But the child was snatched away and
taken to God and his throne. 6 The woman fled to the
desert; there God had prepared a place for her, where she
will be taken care of for twelve hundred and sixty days.

7 Then war broke out in heaven! Michael and his angels
fought against the dragon, who fought back with his angels;

[8] but the dragon was defeated, and he and his angels were
not allowed to stay in heaven any longer. [9] The huge
dragon was thrown out! He is that old serpent, named the
Devil, or Satan, that deceived the whole world. He was
thrown down to earth, and all his angels with him.
[10] Then I heard a loud voice in heaven saying: "Now
God's salvation has come! Now God has shown his power
as King! Now his Messiah has shown his authority! For
the accuser of our brothers, who stood before God accus-
ing them day and night, has been thrown out of heaven.
[11] Our brothers won the victory over him by the blood of
the Lamb, and by the truth which they proclaimed; and
they were willing to give up their lives and die. [12] And
so rejoice, you heavens, and all you who live there! But
how terrible for the earth and the sea! For the Devil
has come down to you, and he is filled with rage, for he
knows that he has only a little time left."
[13] When the dragon realized that he had been thrown
down to the earth, he began to pursue the woman who had
given birth to the boy. [14] The woman was given the two
wings of a large eagle in order to fly to her place in the
desert, where she will be taken care of for three and a half
years, safe from the serpent's attack. [15] Then the serpent
made water pour out of his mouth like a river after the
woman, so that the flood of water would carry her away.
[16] But the earth helped the woman; it opened its mouth
and swallowed the water that had come from the dragon's

mouth. 17 Then the dragon was furious with the woman,
and went off to fight against the rest of her descendants, all
those who obey God's commandments and are faithful to
the truth revealed by Jesus. 18 And the dragon stood on
the seashore.

The Two Beasts

13 Then I saw a beast coming up out of the sea. It
had ten horns and seven heads, with a crown on
each of its horns, and a wicked name written on its heads.
2 The beast I saw looked like a leopard, with feet like a
bear's feet, and a mouth like a lion's mouth. The dragon
gave the beast his own power, his throne, and his vast
authority. 3 One of the heads of the beast seemed to have
been killed, but the fatal wound had healed. The whole
earth was amazed and followed after the beast. 4 All
people worshipped the dragon because he had given his
authority to the beast. They worshipped the beast also,
saying: "Who is like the beast? Who can fight against it?"

5 The beast was allowed to say terribly wicked things,
and it was permitted to have authority for forty-two
months. 6 It began to curse God, and God's name, and
the place where he lives, including all those who live in
heaven. 7 It was allowed to fight against God's people and
to defeat them, and it was given authority over every tribe
and people, every language and nation. 8 All people living
on earth will worship it, that is, everyone whose name has
not been written, before the world began, in the book of
the living that belongs to the Lamb that was killed.

9 "Listen, then, if you have ears to hear with! 10 Who-
ever is meant to be captured, will surely be captured;
whoever is meant to be killed by the sword, will surely
be killed by the sword. This calls for endurance and faith
on the part of God's people."

11 Then I saw another beast coming up out of the earth.
It had two horns like a lamb's horns, and it spoke like a
dragon. 12 It used the vast authority of the first beast in
its presence. It forced the earth and all who live on it to
worship the first beast, whose fatal wound had been healed.
13 This second beast performed great miracles; it made fire
come down out of heaven to earth, in the presence of all
men. 14 And it deceived all the people living on earth by
means of the miracles which it was allowed to perform in

the presence of the first beast. The beast told all the people
of the world to build an image in honour of the beast that
had been wounded by the sword, and yet lived. 15 The
second beast was allowed to breathe life into the image
of the first beast, so that the image could talk and put to
death all those who would not worship it. 16 The beast
forced all men, small and great, rich and poor, slave and
free, to have a mark placed on their right hands and on
their foreheads. 17 No one could buy or sell unless he had
this mark, that is, the beast's name or the number that
stands for the name.

18 This calls for wisdom. Whoever is intelligent can
figure out the meaning of the number of the beast, because
the number stands for a man's name. Its number is six
hundred and sixty-six.

The Song of the Redeemed

14 Then I looked, and there was the Lamb standing on
Mount Zion; with him were a hundred and forty-
four thousand people who have his name and his Father's
name written on their foreheads. 2 And I heard a voice
from heaven that sounded like the roar of a mighty water-
fall, like a loud peal of thunder. The voice I heard
sounded like the music made by harpists playing their
harps. 3 They stood facing the throne and the four living
creatures and the elders, and they sang a new song which
no one could learn except the one hundred and forty-four
thousand people who have been redeemed from the earth.
4 They are the men who have kept themselves pure by not
having relations with women; they are unmarried. They
follow the Lamb wherever he goes; they have been re-
deemed from the rest of mankind and are the first ones to
be offered to God and to the Lamb. 5 They have never
been known to lie; they are without fault.

The Three Angels

6 Then I saw another angel flying high in the air, with
an eternal message of Good News to announce to the
peoples of the earth, to every nation and tribe and language
and people. 7 He said in a loud voice: "Fear God, and
praise his greatness! For the time has come for him to
judge mankind. Bow in worship, then, before God, who
made heaven, earth, sea, and the springs of water!"

8 A second angel followed the first one, saying: "She has
fallen! The great Babylon has fallen! She gave her wine
to all peoples, and made them drink it — the strong wine
of her immoral lust!"
9 A third angel followed the first two, saying in a loud
voice: "Whoever worships the beast and its image, and
receives the mark on his forehead or on his hand, 10 will
himself drink God's wine, the wine of his anger, which he
has poured at full strength into the cup of his wrath! All
who do this will be tormented in fire and sulphur before
the holy angels and the Lamb. 11 The smoke of the fire
that torments them goes up for ever and ever. There is
no relief, day or night, for those who worshipped the beast
and its image, for anyone who received the mark of its
name."
12 This calls for endurance on the part of God's people,
those who obey God's commandments and are faithful to
Jesus.
13 Then I heard a voice from heaven saying: "Write
this: Happy are the dead who from now on die in the
service of the Lord!" "Certainly so," answers the Spirit.
"They will enjoy rest from their hard work; for they take
with them the results of their service."

The Harvest of the Earth

14 Then I looked, and there was a white cloud, and sit-
ting on the cloud was a being who looked like a man, with
a gold crown on his head and a sharp sickle in his hand.
15 Then another angel went out from the temple and cried
out in a loud voice to the one who was sitting on the
cloud: "Use your sickle and reap the harvest, because the

right time has come; the earth is ripe for the harvest!"
16 Then the one who sat on the cloud swung his sickle on
the earth, and the earth's harvest was reaped.

17 Then I saw another angel come out of the temple in
heaven, and he also had a sharp sickle.

18 Then another angel, who is in charge of the fire, came
from the altar. He shouted in a loud voice to the angel
who had the sharp sickle: "Use your sickle, and cut the
grapes from the vineyard of the earth, because the grapes
are ripe!" 19 So the angel swung his sickle on the earth, cut
the grapes from the vine, and threw them into the wine-
press of God's great anger. 20 The grapes were squeezed
out in the winepress outside the city, and blood came out
of the winepress in a flood two hundred miles long and
about five feet deep.

The Angels with the Last Plagues

15 Then I saw another great and amazing sign in
heaven: seven angels with seven plagues. These
are the last plagues, for they are the final expression of
God's wrath.

2 Then I saw what looked like a sea of glass, mixed with
fire; I also saw those who had won the victory over the
beast and its image, and over the one whose name is given
by a number. They were standing by the sea of glass, hold-
ing harps that God had given them. 3 They were singing
the song of Moses, the servant of God, and the song of the
Lamb:

"Lord, God Almighty,
How great and wonderful are your deeds!
King of all nations,
How right and true are your ways!
4 Who will not fear you, Lord?
Who will refuse to declare your greatness?
For you alone are holy.
All the nations will come
And worship before you,
For your righteous deeds are seen by all."

5 After this I saw the temple in heaven open, with the
tent of God's presence in it. 6 The seven angels who had
the seven last plagues came out of the temple; they were
dressed in clean white linen, and had gold bands tied
around their chests 7 Then one of the four living crea-

tures gave the seven angels seven gold bowls full of the
wrath of God, who lives for ever and ever. 8 The temple
was filled with smoke from the glory and power of God,
and no one could go into the temple until the end of the
seven plagues brought by the seven angels.

The Bowls of God's Wrath

16 Then I heard a loud voice speaking from the temple
to the seven angels: "Go and pour out the seven
bowls of God's wrath on the earth!"
2 The first angel went and poured out his bowl on the
earth. Terrible and painful sores appeared on those who
had the mark of the beast, and on those who had wor-
shipped its image.
3 Then the second angel poured out his bowl on the sea.
The water became like the blood of a dead person, and
every living creature in the sea died.
4 Then the third angel poured out his bowl on the rivers
and the springs of water, and they turned into blood. 5 I
heard the angel in charge of the waters say: "You are
righteous in these judgments you have made, O Holy One,
who is and who was! 6 They poured out the blood of God's
people and of the prophets, and so you have given them
blood to drink. They are getting what they deserve!"
7 Then I heard a voice from the altar saying, "Lord, God
Almighty! True and righteous indeed are your judgments!"
8 Then the fourth angel poured out his bowl on the sun,
and it was allowed to burn men with its fiery heat. 9 Men
were burned by the fierce heat, and they cursed the name
of God, who has authority over these plagues; but they
would not turn from their sins and praise his greatness.
10 Then the fifth angel poured out his bowl on the throne
of the beast. Darkness fell over the beast's kingdom,
and men bit their tongues because of their pain, 11 and
they cursed the God of heaven for their pains and sores.
But they did not turn from their evil ways.
12 Then the sixth angel poured out his bowl on the great
river Euphrates. The river dried up, to provide a way for
the kings who come from the east. 13 Then I saw three
unclean spirits, that looked like frogs, coming out of the
mouth of the dragon, the mouth of the beast, and the
mouth of the false prophet. 14 They are the spirits of
demons that perform miracles. These three spirits go out

to the kings over the whole earth, to bring them together
for the war on the great day of Almighty God.
15 "Listen! I am coming like a thief! Happy is he who
stays awake and takes care of his clothing, so that he will
not walk around naked and be ashamed in public!"
16 Then the spirits brought the kings together in the place
that in Hebrew is called Armageddon.
17 Then the seventh angel poured out his bowl in the air.
A loud voice came from the throne in the temple, saying:
"It is done!" 18 There were flashes of lightning, sounds,
peals of thunder, and a terrible earthquake. There never
has been such an earthquake since the creation of man;
this was the worst earthquake of all! 19 The great city was
split into three parts, and the cities of all countries were
destroyed. God remembered great Babylon, and made her
drink the wine from his cup — the wine of his furious
wrath. 20 All the islands disappeared, all the mountains
vanished. 21 Great stones of hail, each weighing as much
as a hundred pounds, fell from the sky on men. And men
cursed God because of the plague of hail, for it was such
a terrible plague.

The Great Prostitute

17 Then one of the seven angels who had the seven
bowls came to me and said: "Come, and I will
show you how the great prostitute is to be punished, that
great city that is built near many rivers. 2 The kings of
the earth committed immorality with the great prostitute,
and the people of the world became drunk from drinking
the wine of her immorality."
3 The Spirit took control of me, and the angel carried
me to a desert. There I saw a woman sitting on a red
beast that had wicked names written all over it; the beast had
seven heads and ten horns. 4 The woman was dressed in
purple and scarlet, covered with gold ornaments, precious
stones, and pearls. In her hand she held a gold cup full of
obscene and filthy things, the result of her immorality.
5 On her forehead was written a name that has a secret
meaning: "The Great Babylon, mother of all prostitutes
and perverts of the world." 6 And I saw that the woman
was drunk with the blood of God's people, and the blood
of those who were killed because they had been loyal to
Jesus.

When I saw her I was completely amazed. 7 "Why are
you amazed?" the angel asked me. "I will tell you the
secret meaning of the woman and of the beast that carries
her, the beast with seven heads and ten horns. 8 The beast
you saw was once alive, but lives no longer; it is about to
come up from the abyss and will go off to be destroyed.
The people living on earth whose names have not been
written, before the world began, in the book of the living,
will all be amazed as they look at the beast. For it was
once alive, but lives no longer, and it will reappear.

9 "This calls for wisdom and understanding. The seven
heads are seven hills, the hills that the woman sits on.
They are also seven kings: 10 five of them have fallen, one
still rules, and the other one has not yet come; when he
comes he must remain only a little while. 11 And the beast
that was once alive, but lives no longer, is itself an eighth
king who belongs to the first seven and goes off to be
destroyed.

12 "The ten horns you saw are ten kings who have not
yet begun to rule, but who will be given authority to rule as
kings for one hour with the beast. 13 These ten all have the
same purpose, and give their power and authority to the
beast. 14 They will fight against the Lamb; but the Lamb,
and his called, chosen, and faithful followers with him, will
defeat them, for he is Lord of lords and King of kings."

15 The angel also said to me: "The waters you saw, on
which the woman sits, are peoples and crowds and nations
and languages. 16 The ten horns you saw, and the beast,
will hate the prostitute; they will take away everything she
has and leave her naked; they will eat her flesh and de-
stroy her with fire. 17 For God placed in their hearts the
desire to carry out his purpose, by acting with one accord
and giving to the beast their power to rule, until God's
words come true.

18 "The woman you saw is the great city that dominates
the kings of the earth."

The Fall of Babylon

18 After this I saw another angel coming down out of
heaven. He had great authority, and his splendour
brightened the whole earth. 2 He cried out in a loud voice:
"She has fallen! The great Babylon has fallen! She is now
haunted by demons and unclean spirits; all kinds of filthy

and hateful birds live in her. 3 For she gave her wine to
all peoples and made them drink it — the strong wine of
her immoral lust. The kings of the earth committed immo-
rality with her, and the businessmen of the world grew
rich from her unrestrained lust."

4 Then I heard another voice from heaven, saying:

"Come out, my people! Come out from her!
You must not take part in her sins,
You must not share her punishments!
5 For her sins are piled up as high as heaven,
And God remembers her wicked ways.
6 Treat her exactly as she has treated you,
Pay her back twice as much as she has done.
Fill her cup with a drink twice as strong
As the drink she prepared for you.
7 Give her as much suffering and grief
As the glory and luxury she gave herself.
For she keeps telling herself:
'Here I sit, a queen!
I am no widow,
I will never know grief!'
8 Because of this her plagues will all strike her
in one day:
Disease, grief, and famine;
She will be burned with fire.
For the Lord God, who judges her, is
mighty."

9 The kings of the earth who shared her immorality and
lust will cry and weep for the city when they see the smoke
of her burning. 10 They stand a long way off, because they
are afraid of her suffering, and say: "How terrible! How
awful! This great and mighty city Babylon! In just one
hour you have been punished!"

11 The businessmen of the earth also cry and mourn for
her, because no one buys their goods any longer; 12 no one
buys their gold, silver, precious stones, and pearls; their
goods of linen, purple cloth, silk, and scarlet; all kinds of
rare woods, and all kinds of objects made of ivory and of
expensive wood, of bronze, iron, and marble; 13 and cinna-
mon, spice, incense, myrrh, and frankincense; wine and
oil, flour and wheat, cattle and sheep, horses and carriages,
slaves and even men's souls. 14 The businessmen say to
her: "All the good things you longed to own have dis-

appeared, and all your wealth and glamour are gone, and
you will never find them again!" 15 The businessmen, who
became rich from doing business in that city, will stand a
long way off, because they are afraid of her suffering.
They will cry and mourn, 16 and say: "How terrible!
How awful for the great city! She used to dress herself in
linen and purple and scarlet, and cover herself with gold
ornaments, precious stones, and pearls! 17 And in one hour
she has lost all this wealth!"

All the ship captains and passengers, the sailors and all
others who earn their living on the sea, stood a long way
off, 18 and cried out as they saw the smoke of her burning:
"There never has been another city like the great city!"
19 They threw dust on their heads, they cried and
mourned: "How terrible! How awful for the great city!
She is the city where all who have ships sailing the seas
became rich on her wealth! And in one hour she has lost
everything!"

20 Rejoice, because of her destruction, O heaven! Re-
joice, God's people, and the apostles and prophets! For
God has judged her for what she did to you!

21 Then a mighty angel picked up a stone the size of a
large millstone and threw it into the sea, saying: "This is
how the great city Babylon will be thrown down with vio-
lence, and will never be seen again. 22 The music of harpists
and musicians, of players of the flute and the trumpet, will
never be heard in you again! No workman in any trade
will ever be found in you again; and the sound of the mill-
stone will be heard no more! 23 Never again will the light
of a lamp be seen in you; no more will the voices of bride
and groom be heard in you. Your businessmen were the
most powerful in all the world, and with your false magic
you deceived all the peoples of the world!"

24 Babylon was punished because the blood of prophets

and of God's people was found in the city; yes, the blood
of all those who have been killed on earth.
19 After this I heard what sounded like the loud voice
of a great crowd of people in heaven, saying:
"Praise God! Salvation, glory, and power belong to our
God! 2 True and righteous are his judgments! For he has
condemned the great prostitute who was corrupting the earth
with her immorality. God has punished her because she
killed his servants." 3 Again they shouted: "Praise God!
The smoke from the burning of the great city goes up for
ever and ever!" 4 The twenty-four elders and the four liv-
ing creatures fell down and worshipped God who was seated
on the throne, and said: "Amen! Praise God!"

The Wedding Feast of the Lamb

5 Then there came from the throne the sound of a voice,
saying: "Praise our God, all his servants, and all men,
both great and small, who fear him!" 6 Then I heard what
sounded like the voice of a great crowd, like the roar of a
mighty waterfall, like loud peals of thunder. I heard them
say: "Praise God! For the Lord, our Almighty God, is
King! 7 Let us rejoice and be glad; let us praise his great-
ness! For the time has come for the wedding of the Lamb,
and his bride has prepared herself for it. 8 She has been
permitted to dress herself with clean shining linen." (The
linen is the righteous deeds of God's people.)
9 Then the angel said to me: "Write this: Happy are
those who have been invited to the wedding feast of the
Lamb." And the angel added, "These are the true words
of God." 10 I fell down at his feet to worship him, but he
said to me: "Don't do it! I am a fellow servant of yours,
and of your brothers, all those who hold to the truth that
Jesus revealed. Worship God!"
For the truth that Jesus revealed is what inspires the
prophets.

The Rider on the White Horse

11 Then I saw heaven open, and there was a white horse.
Its rider is called Faithful and True; it is with justice that
he judges and fights his battles. 12 His eyes were like a
flame of fire, and he wore many crowns on his head. He
had a name written on him, but no one except himself
knows what it is. 13 The robe he wore was covered with

blood. The name by which he is called is "The Word of
God." 14 The armies of heaven followed him, riding on
white horses and dressed in clean white linen. 15 A sharp
sword came out of his mouth, with which he will defeat
the nations. He will rule over them with a rod of iron, and
he will squeeze out the wine in the winepress of the furious
wrath of the Almighty God. 16 On his robe and on his leg
was written the name: "King of kings and Lord of lords."
17 Then I saw an angel standing in the sun. He shouted
in a loud voice to all the birds flying in mid-air: "Come,
and gather together for God's great feast! 18 Come and
eat the flesh of kings, generals, and soldiers, the flesh of
horses and their riders, the flesh of all men, slave and free,
great and small!"
19 Then I saw the beast and the kings of the earth and
their armies gathered to fight against the one who rides the
horse, and against his army. 20 The beast was taken pris-
oner, together with the false prophet who had performed
miracles in his presence. (It was by those miracles that
he had deceived those who had the mark of the beast, and
those who had worshipped the image of the beast.) The
beast and the false prophet were both thrown alive into
the lake of fire that burns with sulphur. 21 Their armies
were killed by the sword that comes out of the mouth of
the one who rides the horse; and all the birds ate all they
could of their flesh.

The Thousand Years

20 Then I saw an angel coming down from heaven,
holding in his hand the key of the abyss, and a heavy

chain. [2] He seized the dragon, that old serpent — that is,
the Devil, or Satan — and tied him up for a thousand
years. [3] The angel threw him into the abyss, locked it and
sealed it, so that he could not deceive the nations any
more until the thousand years were over. After that he
must be set loose for a little while.

[4] Then I saw thrones, and those who sat on them; they
were given the power to judge. I also saw the souls of
those who had been executed because they had proclaimed
the truth that Jesus revealed and the word of God. They
had not worshipped the beast or its image, nor had they
received the mark of the beast on their foreheads or hands.
They lived and ruled as kings with Christ for a thousand
years. [5] (The rest of the dead did not come to life until
the thousand years were over.) This is the first raising
of the dead. [6] Happy and greatly blessed are those who
have a part in this first raising of the dead. The second
death has no power over them; they shall be priests of
God and of Christ, and they will rule with him for a
thousand years.

The Defeat of Satan

[7] After the thousand years are over, Satan will be set
loose from his prison, [8] and he will go out to deceive the
nations scattered over all the world, that is, Gog and
Magog. Satan will bring them all together for battle, as
many as the grains of sand on the seashore. [9] They spread
out over the earth and surrounded the camp of God's
people and the city that he loves. But fire came down from
heaven and destroyed them. [10] Then the Devil, who de-
ceived them, was thrown into the lake of fire and sulphur,
where the beast and the false prophet had already been
thrown; and they will be tormented day and night, for
ever and ever.

The Final Judgment

[11] Then I saw a large white throne and the one who sits
on it. Earth and heaven fled from his presence, and were
seen no more. [12] And I saw the dead, great and small
alike, standing before the throne. Books were opened, and
then another book was opened, the book of the living. The

dead were judged according to what they had done, as was
written in the books. [13] Then the sea gave up its dead.
Death and the world of the dead also gave up the dead
they held. And all were judged according to what they had
done. [14] Then death and the world of the dead were
thrown into the lake of fire. (This lake of fire is the sec-
ond death.) [15] Whoever did not have his name written
in the book of the living was thrown into the lake of fire.

The New Heaven and the New Earth

21 Then I saw a new heaven and a new earth. The
first heaven and the first earth disappeared, and the
sea vanished. [2] And I saw the Holy City, the new Jeru-
salem, coming down out of heaven from God, prepared
and ready, like a bride dressed to meet her husband. [3] I
heard a loud voice speaking from the throne: "Now God's
home is with men! He will live with them, and they shall
be his people. God himself will be with them, and he will
be their God. [4] He will wipe away all tears from their
eyes. There will be no more death, no more grief, crying,
or pain. The old things have disappeared."

[5] Then the one who sits on the throne said, "And now I
make all things new!" He also said to me, "Write this,
because these words are true and can be trusted." [6] And
he said: "It is done! I am the Alpha and the Omega, the
beginning and the end. To anyone who is thirsty I will
give a free drink of water from the spring of the water of
life. [7] Whoever wins the victory will receive this from me:
I will be his God, and he will be my son. [8] But the cow-
ards, the traitors, and the perverts, the murderers and the
immoral, those who practice magic and those who worship
idols, and all liars — the place for them is the lake burning
with fire and sulphur, which is the second death."

The New Jerusalem

[9] One of the seven angels who had the seven bowls full
of the seven last plagues came to me and said, "Come, and
I will show you the Bride, the wife of the Lamb." [10] The
Spirit took control of me, and the angel carried me to the
top of a very high mountain. He showed me Jerusalem, the
Holy City, coming down out of heaven from God, [11] shin-

ing with the glory of God. The city shone like a precious
stone, like a jasper, clear as crystal. 12 It had a great, high
wall, with twelve gates, and with twelve angels in charge of
the gates. On the gates were written the names of the
twelve tribes of the people of Israel. 13 There were three
gates on each side: three on the east, three on the south,
three on the north, and three on the west. 14 The city's
wall was built on twelve stones, on which were written the
names of the twelve apostles of the Lamb.

15 The angel who spoke to me had a gold measuring
stick, to measure the city, its gates, and its wall. 16 The
city was perfectly square, as long as it was wide. The
angel measured the city with his measuring stick: it was
fifteen hundred miles long, and was as wide and as high
as it was long. 17 The angel also measured the wall, and it
was two hundred and sixteen feet high, according to the
normal unit of measure, which he was using. 18 The wall
was made of jasper, and the city itself was made of pure
gold, as clear as glass. 19 The foundation stones of the
city wall were adorned with all kinds of precious stones.
The first foundation stone was jasper, the second sapphire,
the third agate, the fourth emerald, 20 the fifth onyx, the
sixth carnelian, the seventh yellow quartz, the eighth beryl,
the ninth topaz, the tenth chalcedony, the eleventh tur-
quoise, the twelfth amethyst. 21 The twelve gates are
twelve pearls; each gate is made from a single pearl. The
street of the city is of pure gold, transparent as glass.

22 I did not see a temple in the city, because its temple

is the Lord God, the Almighty, and the Lamb. 23 The city
has no need of the sun or the moon to shine on it, for the
glory of God shines on it, and the Lamb is its lamp. 24 The
peoples of the world will walk by its light, and the kings
of the earth will bring their wealth into it. 25 The gates of
the city will stand open all day; they will never be closed,
because there will be no night there. 26 The greatness and
the wealth of the nations will be brought into the city.
27 But nothing that is defiled will enter the city, nor any-
one who does shameful things or tells lies. Only those
whose names are written in the Lamb's book of the living
will enter the city.

22 The angel also showed me the river of the water of
life, sparkling like crystal, which comes from the
throne of God and of the Lamb, 2 and flows down the
middle of the city's street. On each side of the river was
the tree of life, which bears fruit twelve times a year, once
every month; and its leaves are for the healing of the na-
tions. 3 Nothing that is under God's curse will be found in
the city.

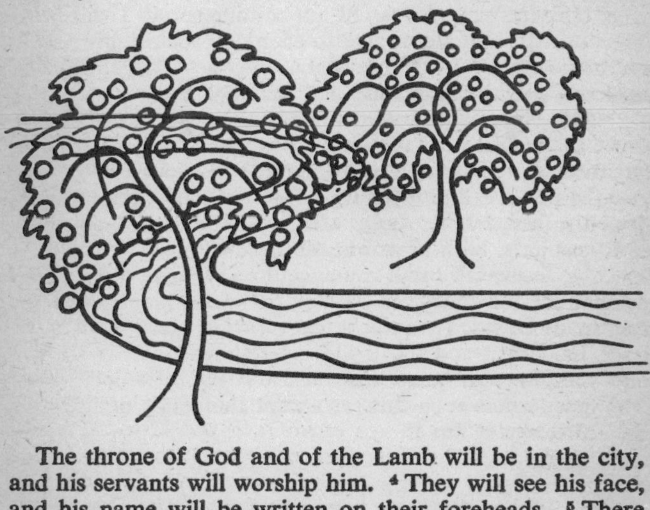

The throne of God and of the Lamb will be in the city,
and his servants will worship him. 4 They will see his face,
and his name will be written on their foreheads. 5 There
shall be no more night, and they will not need lamps or
sunlight, for the Lord God will be their light, and they will
rule as kings for ever and ever.

The Coming of Jesus

6 Then the angel said to me: "These words are true and
can be trusted. And the Lord God, who gives his Spirit to
the prophets, sent his angel to show his servants what must
happen very soon."

7 "Listen!" says Jesus. "I am coming soon! Happy are
those who obey the prophetic words in this book!"

8 I, John, have heard and seen all these things. And
when I finished hearing and seeing them, I fell down at the
feet of the angel who had shown me these things to wor-
ship him. 9 But he said to me: "Don't do it! I am a fellow
servant of yours, and of your brothers the prophets, and of
all those who obey the words in this book. Worship God!"
10 And he said to me: "Do not keep the prophetic words
of this book a secret, for the time is near when all this
will happen. 11 Whoever is evil must go on doing evil,
and whoever is filthy must go on being filthy; whoever is
good must go on doing good, and whoever is holy must go
on being holy."

12 "Listen!" says Jesus. "I am coming soon! I will bring
my rewards with me to give to each one according to what
he has done. 13 I am the Alpha and the Omega, the first
and the last, the beginning and the end."

14 Happy are those who wash their robes clean, and so
have the right to eat the fruit from the tree of life, and to
go through the gates into the city. 15 But outside the city
are the perverts and those who practice magic, the immoral
and the murderers, those who worship idols, and those
who are liars, both in words and deeds.

16 "I, Jesus, have sent my angel to announce these things
to you in the churches. I am the descendant from the
family of David; I am the bright morning star."

17 The Spirit and the Bride say, "Come!"

Everyone who hears this must also say, "Come!"

Come, whoever is thirsty; accept the water of life as a
gift, whoever wants it.

Conclusion

18 I, John, solemnly warn everyone who hears the
prophetic words of this book: if anyone adds anything to
them, God will add to his punishment the plagues described
in this book. 19 And if anyone takes away anything from

the prophetic words of this book, God will take away
from him his share of the fruit of the tree of life, and his
share of the Holy City, which are described in this book.
20 He who gives his testimony to all this, says, "Certainly
so! I am coming soon!"

So be it. Come, Lord Jesus!

21 May the grace of the Lord Jesus be with all.

APPENDICES

APPENDIX A

RECONSTRUCTION OF THE TEXT

One

The French version of the Jerusalem Bible (Les Editions du Cerf, Paris, 1972) proposes that the prophetic part of the Apocalypse – chapters 4 to 22 – is composed of two different Apocalypses 'written by the same author at different dates, and brought together in a single text by a different hand at a later date'. It also maintains that the Letters to the Churches circulated separately. The two primitive texts are composed of the following sections:

	Text I	Text II
Prologue		10:1–2a, 3–4, 8–11
Satan against the Church	12:1–6, 13–17	12:7–12
The Beast against the Church		13
Prologue to the Day of Wrath	4–9; 10:1, 2b, 5–7; 11:14–18	14–16
The Day of Wrath		
Picture of Babylon	17:1–9, 15–18	17:10, 12–14
Fall of Babylon	18:1–3	(cf. 14:8)
The Elect Saved		18:4–8
Threnody on Babylon	18:9–13, 15–19, 21, 24	18:14, 22–23
Triumphal Song	19:1–10	18:20 (cf. 16:5–7)
The Messianic Reign	20:1–6	
Final Conflict	20:7–10	19:11–21
The Judgement	20:13–15	20:11–12
The New Jerusalem	21:9–22, 6–15	21:1–4; 22:3–5, 21:5–8
Appendix: Two Witnesses		11:1–13, 19

Two

Preston and Hanson (pp. 23–24) make rearrangements of chapters 6–16, and 20–22 as follows:

a. The Three Series of Judgements
   i. The seven seals (6)
      Parenthesis: Marking of Saints and Triumph of Redeemed (7)
   ii. The seven trumpets (8–9; 11:14–19; 13)
      Parenthesis: Angel and Book, Temple, and Witnesses (10–11:13)

The seven trumpets, continued (11:14–19)
Parenthesis: Woman, Child, and Dragon (12)
The seven trumpets, continued (13)
Parenthesis: Lamb on Mount, Son of Man in Power (14)
iii. The seven bowls (15–16)

b. The Millennial City, The Last Judgement, the Eternal City, etc.
The Millenial City (20:4–10, 21:7–22:2, 14, 15)
The Last Judgement (20:11–15)
The Eternal City (21:1–6; 22:3–5)
Epilogue (22:6–13, 16–21)

Three

John Oman and T. W. Manson, after an exacting examination of the text, which included the assessment of page-lengths and an attempt to show where they had got out of order in manuscripts, made the following impressive reconstruction:

Section One: The Prophetic Call
1:9–3:22; 10:1–10; 22:6–8; 10:11
Section Two: The Forces in Conflict
11:1–13; 12:1–14:5
Section Three: The Fall of the Monarchies
19:11–16; 14:19–20; 19:17–21; 6:2–17; 15:5–16:16
Section Four: The End of the World Rule
16:17–17:9; 17:10–19:9
Section Five: The Millennial Rule
21:9–23:17; 16:15; 19:9–10; 20:1–10
Section Six: The Last Things
20:10; 4:1–5:2; 5:2–6:1; 7:1–17; 8:1–9:21; 11:14–19; 14:6–11; 14:11–19; 15:1–4; 20:11–21:8
Editor's Introduction: 1:1–8
Editor's Epilogue: 22:18–21

The main Editor's Glosses, it is suggested, are:

1:20; 2:11, 17, 29; 3:6, 13; 11:13; 15:8b; 16:2b; 3b, 6b, 9, 11; 6:3, 5a, 7, 18a, 21b; 7:2b, 5–8; 8:7–12; 22:8–9

Anyone who is sufficiently interested in *Revelation* to be concerned about the original text should try to get hold of this work which, though not easily found in libraries, affords a splendid example of the painstaking scholarship which is brought to bear on the Bible as a whole.

APPENDIX B

SOME FURTHER READING

Revelation, George Caird, A. and C. Black, 1966 – the best recent commentary

Revelation, Moffat Version, Martin Kiddle, Hodder & Stoughton – longish, and prosy, but extremely useful

Revelation, The Interpreter's Bible, Abingdon Press, 1957 – the exegesis, by Martin Rist, is illuminating and scholarly, and particularly good on inter-testamental literature, but the exposition, by Lynn Harold Hough, is baleful

Revelation, John Oman, Cambridge, 1923. Fascinating, though for the specialist.

Revelation, Preston and Hanson, SCM, 1949, revised 1968 – perhaps the best of the short commentaries

Revelation, Matthew Henry, abridged version by David Winter, Hodder and Stoughton, 1975 – old, of course, but not to be neglected, especially by preachers

Revelation, Austin Farrer, published as *The Rebirth of Images*, Dacre Press, 1949 – idiosyncratic to some degree, and not easy reading; an interesting schema, but no references and no bibliography

The Face of the Deep, Christina Rossetti, SPCK, 1892 – a devotional commentary which looks, and is, dense; but is not as forbidding as it looks if taken in short sections

As Seeing the Invisible, D. T. Niles, SCM, 1962 – another devotional work, particularly good on the liturgical structure of *Revelation*

Letters to the Seven Churches, W. M. Ramsey, Hodder and Stoughton, 1906 – excellent, though maybe dated, on the topography of the Asian Churches

Letters to the Seven Churches, William Barclay, SCM, 1957 – a vamped and much condensed version of a great deal of Ramsey's work, with some useful pieces on the Greek words and the customary Barclay sermonettes

The Future of the World, Mathias Rissi, SCM, 1972 – a scholarly and readable account of the last four chapters of *Revelation*

Apocalypse, D. H. Lawrence, Penguin, 1974 – provocative, and right – and wrong!

OTHER BOOKS

The Book of Enoch, translated by R. H. Charles, whose great two-volume work on *Revelation* is in the International Critical Com-

mentary series, and published by SPCK. It is the best example of non-biblical apocalyptic writing
The Primitive Christian Catechism, P. Carrington, Cambridge, 1940
The Sense of an Ending, Frank Kermode, Oxford, 1967 – brilliant
The Death of the Past, J. H. Plumb, Macmillan, 1969 – brilliant and terrifying
In the End God, John Robinson, Fontana, 1968
The End of Time, Josef Pieper, Faber, 1954
Christ and Time, Oscar Cullman, SCM, 1946
The Pursuit of the Millennium, Norman Cohn, Paladin
There are good articles in the new version of Peake's *One-Volume Bible Commentary*, and the new Catholic Encyclopedia

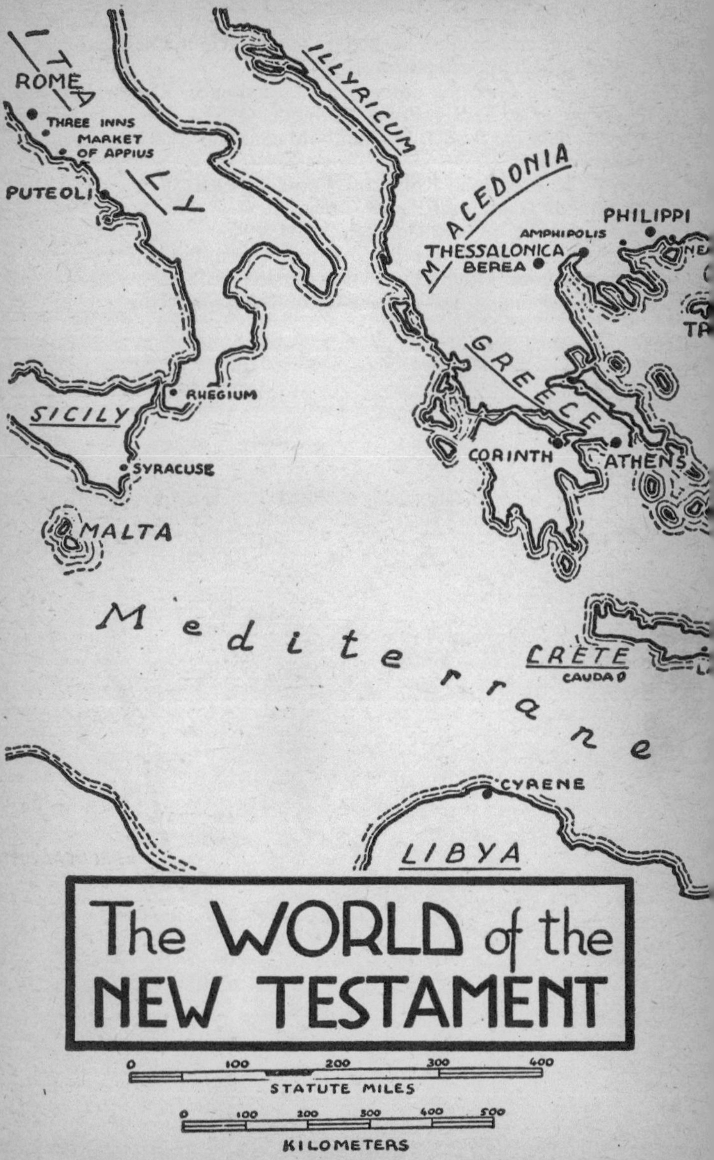
ITALY
ROME
THREE INNS
MARKET OF APPIUS
PUTEOLI
ILLYRICUM
MACEDONIA
PHILIPPI
AMPHIPOLIS
THESSALONICA
BEREA
GREECE
CORINTH
ATHENS
RHEGIUM
SICILY
SYRACUSE
MALTA
Mediterranean
CRETE
CAUDA
CYRENE
LIBYA
The WORLD of the NEW TESTAMENT
0 100 200 300 400
STATUTE MILES
0 100 200 300 400 500
KILOMETERS

Black Sea
BITHYNIA
PONTUS
GALATIA
MYSIA
CAPPADOCIA
PERGAMUM
THYATIRA
ASIA
SMYRNA
SARDIS
PHILADELPHIA
ANTIOCH
EPHESUS
HIERAPOLIS
LAODICEA
COLOSSAE
ICONIUM
LYSTRA
MILETUS
PATMOS
DERBE
TARSUS
PAMPHYLIA
PERGA
ATTALIA
CILICIA
LYCIA
MYRA
ANTIOCH
SYRIA
CAPE SALMONE
CYPRUS
DAMASCUS
SIDON
TYRE
Sea
CAESAREA
JOPPA
PALESTINE
JERUSALEM
GAZA
ALEXANDRIA
EGYPT
ARABIA

THE BIBLE READING FELLOWSHIP

Readers of this commentary may wish to follow a regular pattern of Bible reading, designed to cover the Bible roughly on the basis of a book a month. Suitable Notes (send for details) with helpful exposition and prayers are provided by the Bible Reading Fellowship three times a year (January to April, May to August, September to December), and are available from:—

UK	The Bible Reading Fellowship, St Michael's House, 2 Elizabeth Street, London SW1.W 9RQ.
USA	The Bible Reading Fellowship, P.O. Box 299, Winter Park, Florida 32789, USA.
AUSTRALIA	The Bible Reading Fellowship, Jamieson House, Constitution Avenue, Reid, Canberra, ACT 2601, Australia.